Ecclesiology

Understanding God's Church

Gregory Brown

BiG
Publishing

Endorsements

"The Bible Teacher's Guide … will help any teacher study and get a better background for his/her Bible lessons. In addition, it will give direction and scope to teaching of the Word of God. Praise God for this contemporary introduction to the Word of God."

—Dr. Elmer Towns
Co-founder of Liberty University
Former Dean, Liberty Baptist Theological Seminary

"Expositional, theological, and candidly practical! I highly recommend The Bible Teacher's Guide for anyone seeking to better understand or teach God's Word."

—Dr. Young–Gil Kim
Founding President, Handong Global University

"Helpful to both the layman and the serious student, The Bible Teacher's Guide, by Dr. Greg Brown, is outstanding!"

—Dr. Neal Weaver
President, Louisiana Baptist University

"Whether you are preparing a Bible study, a sermon, or simply wanting to dive deeper into a personal study of God's Word, these will be very helpful tools."

—Eddie Byun
Associate Professor of Christian Ministry, Biola University
Author of Justice Awakening

"I am happy that Greg is making his insights into God's truth available to a wider audience through these books. They bear the hallmarks of good Bible teaching: the result of rigorous Bible study and thoroughgoing application to the lives of people."

—Ajith Fernando
Teaching Director, Youth for Christ
Author of A Call to Joy and Pain

"The content of the series is rich. My prayer is that God will use it to help the body of Christ grow strong."

—Dr. Min Chung
Senior Pastor, Covenant Fellowship Church, Urbana, Illinois
Adjunct Professor, Urbana Theological Seminary

"Knowing the right questions to ask and how to go about answering them is fundamental to learning in any subject matter. Greg demonstrates this convincingly."

—Dr. William Moulder
Professor of Biblical Studies, Trinity International University

"Pastor Greg is passionate about the Word of God, rigorous and thorough in his approach to the study of it... I am pleased to recommend The Bible Teacher's Guide to anyone who hungers for the living Word."

—Dr. JunMo Cho
Professor of Linguistics, Handong Global University
Contemporary Christian Music Recording Artist

"I can't imagine any student of Scripture not benefiting by this work."

—Steven J. Cole
Pastor, Flagstaff Christian Fellowship, Flagstaff, Arizona
Author of the Riches from the Word series

"Greg deals with the principles, doctrines, and applications of the text in a practical way which is useful for both individual growth or for help in preparation for teaching."

—Bob Deffinbaugh
Ministry Coordinator, Bible.org
Founding Pastor, Community Bible Chapel, Richardson, Texas

Content

Preface

And entrust what you heard me say in the presence of many others as witnesses to faithful people who will be competent to teach others as well.
2 Timothy 2:2 (NET)

Paul's words to Timothy still apply to us today. The church needs teachers who clearly and fearlessly teach the Word of God. With this in mind, The Bible Teacher's Guide (BTG) series was created. This series includes both expositional and topical studies, with resources to help teachers lead small groups, pastors prepare sermons, and individuals increase their knowledge of God's Word.

Ecclesiology can be used for personal study or as a six to eight-session small group curriculum, depending on how the leader divides up the topics. For small groups, the members will read a chapter (or chapters) and discuss the reflection questions and anything else that stood out in the reading within their gathering. Or, the chapter can be read before the gathering, with the meeting focusing only on discussion.

Introduction

Ecclesiology is the study of the church. The church is not a building; it is God's people throughout the world. God has chosen the church to be his global representative (Matt 28:19) and to glorify him throughout eternity (Eph 3:21). The church is God's temple (1 Cor 3:16) and his family (Gal 6:10). It is Christ's body, including various members with different spiritual gifts (1 Cor 12:12-28). It is the salt and light of the world (Matt 5:13-14). While on earth, Christ promised to build his church and that the gates of hades will not prevail against it (Matt 16:18). It is the most important institution in the world. Therefore, as the church goes, the world goes. If the church is healthy, it positively impacts society, and if it is unhealthy, it negatively impacts society. Therefore, what we believe about the church is very important. Let's study it together with the Bible Teacher's Guide. May God the Father, Christ the Son, and the Holy Spirit richly bless your study!

What Is the Church

What is the church? The English word "church" comes from the Greek word "ekklesia," which means "a gathering" or "an assembly" or literally "called-out-ones." It was a word used of any gathering or congregation—not only a religious one. In Matthew 16:18, Christ used it when describing a future congregation of people he would gather. He said, "And I tell you that you are Peter, and on this rock I will build my church, and the gates of Hades will not overpower it." This church would be full of people who God "called out" from the world to be Christ's disciples. In John 6:37-39, Christ said this:

> Everyone whom the Father gives me will come to me, and the one who comes to me I will never send away. For I have come down from heaven not to do my own will but the will of the one who sent me. Now this is the will of the one who sent me—that I should not lose one person of every one he has given me, but raise them all up at the last day.

Also, in John 17:1-2 and 15-18, Christ said this in his high priestly prayer before going to the cross:

> ... Father, the time has come. Glorify your Son, so that your Son may glorify you—just as you have given him authority over all humanity, so that he may give eternal life to everyone you have given him ... I am not asking you to

take them out of the world, but that you keep them safe from the evil one. They do not belong to the world just as I do not belong to the world. Set them apart in the truth; your word is truth. Just as you sent me into the world, so I sent them into the world

Christ described those God gave him (his disciples) as in the world but not "of" the world. The "in" but not "of" demonstrates that the church, though in the world, would be vastly different from the world—in their speech, actions, values, and motivations. It consists of those who have repented of their sins and believed in Christ as their Lord and Savior (John 3:16, Acts 2:38, Rom 10:9-10). In repenting, they have turned away from living for the world (and themselves) to live for Christ. They have been called out of the world to be a blessing to the world. In Matthew 5:13-16, Christ said this to his disciples:

> You are the salt of the earth. But if salt loses its flavor, how can it be made salty again? It is no longer good for anything except to be thrown out and trampled on by people. You are the light of the world. A city located on a hill cannot be hidden. People do not light a lamp and put it under a basket but on a lampstand, and it gives light to all in the house. In the same way, let your light shine before people, so that they can see your good deeds and give honor to your Father in heaven.

Inhabitants

Who are the inhabitants of the church? Though it has a simple answer, like "those who repent of their sins and believe in Christ as their Lord and Savior," it is more complicated than that. Historically, there has been great debate over this question.

Some would say the church includes believers in God from all time periods, including Old Testament believers and specifically those in the nation of Israel. (1) They would say this because some texts use the Greek word "ekklesia" to describe Israel in the Old Testament. For example, in Acts 7:38, Luke wrote about Moses and Israel in the wilderness: "This is the man who was in the congregation in the wilderness with the angel who spoke to him at Mount Sinai, and with our ancestors, and he received living oracles to give to you." "Congregation" is the same word "ekklesia" which is used for "church." Also, Hebrews 2:12, which is a quote by Christ from Psalm 22:22 says, "I will declare your name to my countrymen! In the middle of the assembly I will praise you!" The word "assembly," which in the context of the Psalms probably referred to Israel, is the Greek word "ekklesia."[1]

(2) In addition, throughout the New Testament, the same terminology that was used to describe ethnic Israel is commonly used of the church, often prompting people to call the church the "new Israel" or "spiritual Israel." For example, in Galatians 3:29, Paul says: "And if you belong to Christ, then you are Abraham's descendants, heirs according to the promise." Also, in Romans 4:11, Abraham is called "the father of all those who believe." Therefore, though not physical descendants of Abraham, like Israel, the church is a spiritual descendant because they have Abraham's faith in God and because they belong to Christ—the ultimate seed of Abraham (Gal 3:16). Therefore, it is commonly believed that spiritual Israel, the church, inherits all the promises of physical Israel. This view is often called "replacement" theology (or supersessionism). Likewise, in 1 Peter 2:9, Peter says this about the church: "But you are a chosen race, a royal priesthood, a holy nation, a people of his own, so that you may proclaim the virtues." These are all things originally said about Israel, which gives further evidence to the church being the new Israel (cf. Ex 19:5-6, Dt 7:6, 14:2, etc.). With that said, many only see these texts as showing similarities between the church and Israel as they are both God's

people. Israel was God's instrument in the Old Testament to draw people to the Lord, and the church (which includes believing Jews) is God's instrument in the New.

(3) Furthermore, there are several texts, it is argued, which refer to the church as a continuation of Israel or replacing Israel in God's plan. For example, Romans 2:28-29 says:

> For a person is not a Jew who is one outwardly, nor is circumcision something that is outward in the flesh, but someone is a Jew who is one inwardly, and circumcision is of the heart by the Spirit and not by the written code. This person's praise is not from people but from God.

Here, it is said that Paul is broadening the understanding of a Jew. True Jews are not ethnic, but those who have been transformed spiritually, including Jew and Gentile. William Barclay said this about Paul's words:

> Jewishness, he insists, is not a matter of race at all; it has nothing to do with circumcision. It is a matter of conduct. If that is so, many a so-called Jew, who is a pure descendant of Abraham and who bears the mark of circumcision on his body, is no Jew at all; and equally, many Gentiles, who never heard of Abraham and who would never dream of being circumcised, are Jews in the real sense of the term. To Jews, this would sound like the wildest heresy and leave them angry and aghast.[2]

However, many disagree with this interpretation. They would say that Paul is not broadening who a true Jew is, but narrowing it to saved Jews within the nation of Israel. Christ at times did the same thing in the Gospels. With the Jews who wanted to kill him, he claimed they were not true children of Abraham. John 8:38-39 details this:

They answered him, "Abraham is our father!" Jesus replied, "If you are Abraham's children, you would be doing the deeds of Abraham. But now you are trying to kill me, a man who has told you the truth I heard from God. Abraham did not do this!

Only Jews who practice Abraham's faith are true Jews. Likewise, Christ spoke of other Jews as being true children of Abraham—meaning that they were saved. After Zacchaeus repented of his sins by declaring he would give half of his wealth to the poor and repay those he had cheated, Christ said to him: "Today salvation has come to this household, because he too is a son of Abraham!" (Lk 19:9). He was a true Jew. Likewise, Christ said the same thing to the woman who had been bent over for eighteen years because of a demonic spirit. She was a "daughter of Abraham" (Lk 13:16)—referring to her being truly saved. It is unlikely that Christ was broadening the definition of a child of Abraham at that time since he originally was "sent only to the lost sheep of Israel" (Matt 15:24; cf. Rom 1:16).

Like Christ referring to a true remnant of believers in Israel (Lk 19:9, 13:16, Rev 2:9, 3:9), in Romans 2:28-29, Paul seems to be doing the same. A true Jew is one inwardly and not outwardly—referring to Jewish believers within the nation of Israel. Further evidence for this is the fact that Paul continually refers to the nation of Israel as a separate entity from the church throughout Romans (Chapters 9-11).

Likewise, the same argument is made about Romans 9:6. In it, Paul says, "...For not all those who are descended from Israel are truly Israel." It is argued that when Paul speaks of some being "truly Israel," he is referring to the church, not ethnic, believing Israelites. However, in the context, Paul is arguing that God is not done with ethnic Israel. In Romans 9:3-6, he says:

For I could wish that I myself were accursed—cut off from Christ—for the sake of my people, my fellow countrymen, who are Israelites. To them belong the adoption as sons, the glory, the covenants, the giving of the law, the temple worship, and the promises. To them belong the patriarchs, and from them, by human descent, came the Christ, who is God over all, blessed forever! Amen. It is not as though the word of God had failed. For not all those who are descended from Israel are truly Israel.

Paul will later definitively argue that God is not done with ethnic Israel as they are God's elect and God's gift and call are irrevocable. In fact, all of Israel will be saved at Christ's return. Romans 11:26-29 says:

And so all Israel will be saved, as it is written: "The Deliverer will come out of Zion; he will remove ungodliness from Jacob. And this is my covenant with them, when I take away their sins." In regard to the gospel they are enemies for your sake, but in regard to election they are dearly loved for the sake of the fathers. For the gifts and the call of God are irrevocable.

Again, it seems that in Romans 2:28-29 and 9:6, Paul is referring to Jewish Christians within Israel as being "true Israel" or "true Jews." He was not saying that the church is the new Israel, nor that God has removed his promises to ethnic Israel. Paul actually argues the opposite of that.

Another verse commonly cited by those who see the church as a continuation of Old Testament Israel is Galatians 6:16, which says, "And all who will behave in accordance with this rule, peace and mercy be on them, and on the Israel of God." Depending on how one translates this verse, it could either be distinguishing between Gentile believers and Jewish believers or only speaking of one group—the church as the Israel of God. The NET translation, "and on the Israel of God," distinguishes between Gentile and Jewish Christians, as they are separated by the conjunction "and." The NIV translation, "Peace and mercy to all who follow this rule—to the Israel of God" seems to support the church as being "the Israel of God." There is obviously merit for both translations; however, when studying how the term Israel is used throughout the Old and New Testament to refer to national Israel, it seems best to interpret "Israel of God" as referring to Jewish believers. John MacArthur in his book Bible Doctrine said this:

> Of the more than two thousand uses of the term Israel in Scripture, more than seventy are found in the New Testament. Biblical commentators agree that most of these occurrences refer to ethnic Israel (either the nation as a whole or a group of Jewish people). However, some contend that on certain occasions the New Testament authors apply the name Israel to the church. Yet when the passages in question are studied carefully, it becomes evident that only ethnic Israelites are in view. Consequently, a compelling case can be made to demonstrate that, whenever the New Testament writers use the term Israel, they reserve it exclusively for national Israel.[3]

The view that sees the church including all believers of all times, including Old Testament believers, has been a common view throughout history in both Protestant and Catholic theology.[4] It sees the church and Israel as the same, the church as an expansion or fulfillment of Israel, or even replacing Israel altogether. God has one people group who he is expanding his kingdom through—not two. Therefore, all of God's promises to national Israel are ultimately fulfilled in the church, which now consists of believing Jews and Gentiles. Promises such as Israel eternally having a land, a Davidic king that rules from Jerusalem, a millennial temple, nations coming to worship in Jerusalem, and ethnic Israel being a blessing to all nations, in this view, all symbolize the church in some way.

The view that sees the church including only New Testament believers (Jews and Gentiles together as one entity) is called the dispensational view, which is probably the most popular view in American evangelicalism today.[5] They would see Israel and the church as separate entities with many similarities, such as being children of Abraham (Rom 4:11-12), but with different blessings and callings from God. Israel's promises are commonly earthly, such as having a land, them blessing the nations, and Christ ruling over them and the world from Jerusalem. According to dispensationalism, God will ultimately restore Israel to himself (Rom 11:25-27) and fulfill his promises to her in the millennial kingdom (Is 65, Rev 20). The church's promises are more commonly heavenly, such as being seated with Christ in heaven (Eph 2:6), having every spiritual blessing in heavenly places (Eph 1:3), being the body of Christ (1 Cor 12:13), and eventually ruling with Christ, as his bride, in heaven and on earth (Rev 19:6-7, Lk 19:16-19).

(1) Support for the belief that the church includes only New Testament believers is the fact that Scripture speaks of it as something new—not existing in the past. For example, in Matthew 16:18, Christ said that he would "build" his church. The future tense suggests that the church was something new and not a continuation of something old. Also, in Ephesians 3:2-6, Paul calls the formation of the church as Jewish and Gentile fellow heirs a "divine secret" or "mystery" which was revealed to him and not to "former generations." Certainly, it was always God's plan for Israel to be a light to the Gentiles and a blessing to them, but Israel becoming one with Gentiles in the church and fellow heirs was never clearly revealed. In Ephesians 2:15, Paul describes how Christ "created in himself one new man out of two"—referring to

believing Jews and Gentiles being the church. Since the church is a "new man" and not a continuation of something previously existing, this again suggests the church did not exist in the Old Testament.

(2) Additional evidence that the church is a separate entity from Israel and other Old Testament believers is the description of present heavenly worshipers in Hebrews 12:22-23. It says:

> But you have come to Mount Zion, the city of the living God, the heavenly Jerusalem, and to myriads of angels, to the assembly and congregation of the firstborn, who are enrolled in heaven, and to God, the judge of all, and to the spirits of the righteous, who have been made perfect,

In this heavenly description of worship, it separates angels, the church, and the spirits of the righteous men made perfect. The righteous made perfect seems to clearly refer to Old Testament saints, including Israel, while the church refers to New Testament believers who came to faith after Christ's death and resurrection.

(3) Another evidence that the church began in the New Testament and does not include Old Testament saints is the fact that the body of Christ, which is equivalent to the church (Rom 12:5, 1 Cor 12:27), was not formed until the Holy Spirit was given at Pentecost after Christ's ascension (Acts 2). In 1 Corinthians 12:12-13, Paul says:

> For just as the body is one and yet has many members, and all the members of the body—though many—are one body, so too is Christ. For in one Spirit we were all baptized into one body. Whether Jews or Greeks or slaves or free, we were all made to drink of the one Spirit.

Likewise, it was after Christ's resurrection and ascension that he became the head of the church. After describing how God resurrected Christ and seated him in the heavenlies (Eph 1:20-21), Paul said this: "And God put all things under Christ's feet, and he gave him to the church as head over all things. Now the church is his body, the fullness of him who fills all in all" (Eph 1:22-23). In the Old Testament, believers in God associated with Israel; however, in the New Testament, believers become part of Christ's body, which was formed when the Holy Spirit came at Pentecost (Acts 2). Charles Ryrie summarizes this concept:

> Though there is a continuity between the redeemed of all ages (simply because they are redeemed and their common destiny is heaven), there is a discontinuity because redeemed today are placed in the body of Christ and not in some sort of Israel. Similarly the redeemed before Abraham's day (like Enoch and Noah) did not belong to Israel, yet they belonged to the family of God. So there are pre-Israel redeemed (pre-Abrahamic saints) and post-Israel saints (Christians in the body of Christ).[6]

(4) Finally, as mentioned previously, of the seventy plus times the term Israel is used in the New Testament, most clearly refer to national Israel, and of the few times that some believe it refers to the church as "spiritual Israel" or the "Israel of God," there are compelling arguments that those also refer to ethnic Israelites, albeit believing ones.[7] Consequently, it appears that the church does not include Old Testament believers; it is a formation of believing Jews and Gentiles who have been included in the body of Christ since the coming of the Spirit at Pentecost (cf. Acts 2, 1 Cor 12:13).

With all that said, though Israel and the church may be different, they are both part of God's plan to establish his eternal kingdom and are both part of God's people.[8] The heavenly Jerusalem, which will descend to earth in the eternal stage, will have twelve gates with the names of the twelve tribes of Israel and twelve foundations with the names of the apostles (Rev 21:12-13)—representing both Israel and the church. Ultimately, God's people from all ages will glorify the Lord in his kingdom throughout eternity.

Origin

If the church didn't exist in the Old Testament, when was it formed? In 1 Corinthians 12:13-14, Paul said this:

> For in one Spirit we were all baptized into one body. Whether Jews or Greeks or slaves or free, we were all made to drink of the one Spirit. For in fact the body is not a single member, but many.

Paul's description in 1 Corinthians 12:13 of believers being baptized with one Spirit into the body of Christ indicates that the church began and was formed at Pentecost in Acts 2. Before ascending to heaven, Christ told his disciples to wait in Jerusalem until they were empowered and baptized with God's Spirit. In Acts 1:4-5, Christ said this:

> Do not leave Jerusalem, but wait there for what my Father promised, which you heard about from me. For John baptized with water, but you will be baptized with the Holy Spirit not many days from now.

Then, in Acts 2:4, God's Spirit baptized the disciples, and they spoke in new tongues, symbolizing the new work that God began with his church (cf. Acts 11:15-16). Through Spirit baptism, God formed the body of Christ, which would be Christ's visible witness on the earth. After being baptized with power from above, Peter preached to a great multitude gathered for Pentecost, saying, "Repent, and each one of you be baptized in the name of Jesus

Christ for the forgiveness of your sins, and you will receive the gift of the Holy Spirit" (Acts 2:38). Three thousand responded—forming the first local church, which resided in Jerusalem. As people repented and followed Christ, they immediately became part of the body of Christ, the church.

As often considered, the church did not begin with saints in the Old Testament but with believers at Pentecost, as Jews who repented and believed in Christ were baptized with the Spirit into the newly formed body of Christ (1 Cor 12:13). Later, Gentiles began to follow Christ and became part of his church (Acts 8 and 10). The church is Jew and Gentile believers unified, empowered, and sanctified by God's Spirit in order to glorify God, serve one another, and reach the world for Christ, as his visible representation.

Invisible and Visible

Scripture teaches that the church is both invisible and visible. In what ways is the church invisible? Ephesians 2:6 says, "And he raised us up with him and soated us with him in the heavenly realms in Christ Jesus." When a person is born again by faith in Christ, they are spiritually raised and seated in heavenly places with Christ. God reckons believers as his Son and the privileges and positions he has, they have, since they are his body (1 Cor 12:13). This is demonstrated in the commonly repeated phrase throughout the New Testament epistles, "in Christ." Ephesians 1:3 says, "Blessed is the God and Father of our Lord Jesus Christ, who has blessed us with every spiritual blessing in the heavenly realms in Christ." Second Corinthians 5:17 says, "So then, if anyone is in Christ, he is a new creation; what is old has passed away—look, what is new has come!" Hebrews 12:22-23 describes this spiritual reality of believers being seated in heaven with Christ. It says,

But you have come to Mount Zion, the city of the living God, the heavenly Jerusalem, and to myriads of angels, to the assembly and congregation of the firstborn, who are enrolled in heaven, and to God, the judge of all, and to the spirits of the righteous, who have been made perfect,

This describes the spiritual reality of the invisible church, seated in heavenly places with Christ. The invisible church includes all born again believers, including those alive on earth and those deceased, awaiting their resurrected bodies in heaven.

With that said, Scripture also talks about a visible church, which would not only include born again believers but also professing believers who are not born again. In Matthew 7:21-23, Christ described this unfortunate reality. He said:

"Not everyone who says to me, 'Lord, Lord,' will enter the kingdom of heaven—only the one who does the will of my Father in heaven. On that day, many will say to me, 'Lord, Lord, didn't we prophesy in your name, and in your name cast out demons and do many powerful deeds?' Then I will declare to them, 'I never knew you. Go away from me, you lawbreakers!'

Christ describes how there are many in the church, sometimes even serving and leading in congregations, who are deceived about their salvation. They call him, "Lord" but are not truly saved—their life of iniquity proves this reality.

Likewise, in the Parable of the Wheat and the Weeds, Christ describes this. In Matthew 13:36-43, he said:

Then he left the crowds and went into the house. And his disciples came to him saying, "Explain to us the parable of the weeds in the field." He answered, "The one who sowed the good seed is the Son of Man. The field is the world and the good seed are the people of the kingdom. The weeds are the people of the evil one, and the enemy who sows them is the devil. The harvest is the end of the age, and the reapers are angels. As the weeds are collected and burned with fire, so it will be at the end of the age. The Son of Man will send his angels, and they will gather from his kingdom everything that causes sin as well as all lawbreakers. They will throw them into the fiery furnace, where there will be weeping and gnashing of teeth. Then the righteous will shine like the sun in the kingdom of their Father. The one who has ears had better listen!

In the kingdom of God—the place of God's rule—Christ has planted good seed, representing true believers, and the enemy, the devil, has planted weeds, who are not truly saved. Planting weeds amongst wheat was not an uncommon practice in ancient societies when an enemy was trying to sabotage another person's harvest. The weeds would choke the wheat, hinder growth, and possibly destroy the harvest. That's what Satan has tried to do with Christ's church.

Other parables demonstrate this current state of God's kingdom as well. In the Parable of the Net (Matt 13:47-50), Christ describes the kingdom as a great net that fishermen threw into the sea, catching both good fish and bad fish. The good fish are kept, and the bad fish are burned. Christ said that's how it will be at the end of the age, as the angels throw false believers into the furnace. Likewise, in the Parable of the Virgins (Matt 25:1-13), there were five virgins with oil and five virgins without. When the bridegroom returned, the virgins with oil entered the wedding banquet, but the others, who called the bridegroom, "Lord, Lord," were left out. The bridegroom told them, "I do not know you" (Matt 25:11). In addition, in the Parable of the Sheep and the Goats (Matt 25:31-46), Christ described his return to earth. Those who cared for the least of these, including the hungry, the imprisoned, and those without clothes, were the sheep who entered the kingdom. As they served the least, they served Christ. However, those who neglected the needy were goats. They were rejected from the kingdom and sent into eternal fire (v. 41), though they called Christ, "Lord" (v. 37).

This is the visible church—full of true believers and false believers. Because of this reality, in 2 Corinthians 13:5, Paul said to the Corinthians, "Put yourselves to the test to see if you are in the faith; examine yourselves! Or do you not recognize regarding yourselves that Jesus Christ is in you—unless, indeed, you fail the test!" Likewise, in 2 Peter 1:10, Peter said this to believers: "Therefore, my brothers, make every effort to be sure of your calling and election. For by doing this you will never stumble into sin."

Believers must test the reality of their faith by discerning their fruits (cf. 1 John 5:13, Matt 7:16). Has their profession provoked them to a life of obedience to God's Word? Or, are they calling Christ, "Lord," but not living for him? In Matthew 7:21, Christ said only those who did his Father's will would enter the kingdom. Also, in verse 23, Christ told the professing believers who were serving in leadership within the church, "Depart from me, you workers of iniquity, I never knew you!" (paraphrase). Though they had religion, they had no relationship with Christ, and their profession had never changed their relationship with sin.

The church is both invisible and visible. The invisible church is seated in heavenly places with Christ and includes only true believers; but the visible church includes both true and false believers.

Local, Regional, and Universal

The church is also local, regional, and universal. At times, the word "church" is used in the New Testament to describe a local church, churches in a city or region, or the universal church consisting of all believers. Consider how Paul addressed the Corinthian church in 1 Corinthians 1:1-2:

> From Paul, called to be an apostle of Christ Jesus by the will of God, and Sosthenes, our brother, to the church of God that is in Corinth, to those who are sanctified in Christ Jesus, and called to be saints, with all those in every place who call on the name of our Lord Jesus Christ, their Lord and ours.

Clearly, there were many churches in the city of Corinth, but he addressed them all as "the church of God that is in Corinth." In 1 Corinthians 16:19, Paul spoke about the churches in a region of Asia and a local church which met in Aquila's and Priscilla's house. He said, "The churches in the province of Asia send greetings to you. Aquila and Prisca greet you warmly in the Lord, with the church that meets in their house." In Ephesians 5:25, Paul spoke about the universal church, including all true believers. He said, "Husbands, love your wives, just as Christ loved the church and gave himself for her."

As we consider the fact that the church is local, regional, and universal, it should reinforce our commitment to all three. As believers, we should not be content to be a part of the universal church, we should be committed to a local body of believers. Hebrews 10:25 says, "Not abandoning our own meetings, as some are in the habit of doing, but encouraging each other, and even more so because you see the day drawing near." By being together and serving together, we mutually encourage one another, as we await the Lord's coming. In addition, since a local church is part of the church in a city or region, they should not be isolated or competitive, but seek to pray together, serve together, and reach that city or region for Christ.

Finally, since all true believers are part of the universal church, we must remember and seek to serve the universal church.

In Ephesians 6:18, Paul said, "With every prayer and petition, pray at all times in the Spirit, and to this end be alert, with all perseverance and requests for all the saints." If the church in a certain nation is experiencing revival, we should give thanks and pray for it to continue. If the church in another area is being persecuted, we must mourn and pray for protection and justice. If the church in a specific city has needs, we should pray and seek to help in practical ways, if at all possible.

As believers, we must be committed to the church, which is local, regional, and universal. Christ is the head of the church for whom he gave his life. As he continually loves, serves, and prays for her (cf. Eph 5:25-26, Heb 7:25), so must we. He said they will know we are his disciples by the way we love one another (John 13:35).

Reflection

1. What stood out most in the reading and why?
2. Is the church and Israel the same? Why or why not?
3. In what ways is the church invisible and visible?
4. What applications can we take from the fact that the church is mentioned in Scripture as local, regional, and universal?
5. What other questions or applications did you take from the reading?

Metaphors of the Church

In the New Testament, there are at least eight metaphors used of believers and the church in general, which tell us something about God's purposes for the church. We will consider each one and its applications:

1. The church is pictured as salt.

In Matthew 5:13, Christ said this to his disciples: "You are the salt of the earth. But if salt loses its flavor, how can it be made salty again? It is no longer good for anything except to be thrown out and trampled on by people." Salt was very valuable in ancient times. It was even used as payment for work. This is where the saying, "He is not worth his salt!" comes from. Christ was saying his church and the disciples within it would be very valuable to the world. Part of the reason salt was so valuable was because it was used as a seasoning, but more importantly, it was used as a preservative. Since they did not have refrigerators in ancient times, they would often use a saline solution to preserve food and keep it from decay.

In what ways does the church function as a preservative for the world? (1) As believers live righteous lives, pray, and share the gospel, they keep society from decaying morally and spiritually. This happens because righteous living influences others towards righteousness and staves off ungodliness. First Peter 2:11-12 says,

> Dear friends, I urge you as foreigners and exiles to keep
> away from fleshly desires that do battle against the soul,
> and maintain good conduct among the non-Christians, so
> that though they now malign you as wrongdoers, they may
> see your good deeds and glorify God when he appears.

The implication from Peter's exhortation is that as believers live holy lives, nonbelievers may at times mock them and even persecute them; however, some will eventually accept Christ and glorify God when Christ returns because of his people's righteous example and witness. Though believers are often mocked, rejected, and mistreated, they are needed. Their saltiness positively influences society and holds back moral decay.

(2) Also, in being righteous, believers hold back Gods' wrath from the world. We get a great picture of this when God promised Abraham, he would not destroy Sodom if only ten righteous people were found in it (Gen 18:32). In addition, in Ezekiel 22:30, God promised that if he could find one person to pray for the land, he wouldn't destroy it. It says, "I looked for a man from among them who would repair the wall and stand in the gap before me on behalf of the land, so that I would not destroy it, but I found no one."

2. The church is pictured as light.

In Matthew 5:14, Christ said to his disciples, "You are the light of the world." John MacArthur's comments on the figurative use of light are helpful. He said:

> In Scripture the figurative use of light has two aspects, the
> intellectual and the moral. Intellectually it represents truth,
> whereas morally it represents holiness … The figure of
> darkness has the same two aspects. Intellectually it

represents ignorance and falsehood, whereas morally it connotes evil.[1]

We see this in many places. Psalms 119:105 says, "Your word is a lamp to walk by, and a light to illumine my path." Here light refers to intellectual truth as seen in God's Word. In Romans 13:12-14, it refers to moral deeds, and darkness refers to immoral deeds. It says,

> The night has advanced toward dawn; the day is near. So then we must lay aside the works of darkness, and put on the weapons of light. Let us live decently as in the daytime, not in carousing and drunkenness, not in sexual immorality and sensuality, not in discord and jealousy. Instead, put on the Lord Jesus Christ, and make no provision for the flesh to arouse its desires.

Light exposes darkness and gives off light, brightening a room or space. Therefore, in an intellectual sense, the church exposes lies, gets rid of them, and promotes truth. As the world continually loses a grip on truth, as relativism rules in our day, the church holds to it, as taught in Scripture. In 1 Timothy 3:15 (NIV), Paul called the church "the pillar and foundation of the truth." Also, in a moral sense, as right becomes wrong and wrong becomes right in the world, the church exposes and condemns evil and promotes and practices righteousness. The church is the light of the world!

3.   The church is pictured as a body.

In 1 Corinthians 12:13-18, Paul says:

---

[1] MacArthur, J. F., Jr. (1986). Ephesians (pp. 205–206). Chicago: Moody Press.

For in one Spirit we were all baptized into one body. Whether Jews or Greeks or slaves or free, we were all made to drink of the one Spirit. For in fact the body is not a single member, but many. If the foot says, "Since I am not a hand, I am not part of the body," it does not lose its membership in the body because of that. And if the ear says, "Since I am not an eye, I am not part of the body," it does not lose its membership in the body because of that. If the whole body were an eye, what part would do the hearing? If the whole were an ear, what part would exercise the sense of smell? But as a matter of fact, God has placed each of the members in the body just as he decided.

The metaphor of the church being a body tells us several things: (1) It teaches that believers are interdependent upon one another. Again, Paul said, the eye can't replace the role of the ear, and the ear can't replace the role of the nose. We need to see, hear, and smell. All three are necessary. Likewise, God has gifted believers differently—one may be a teacher, another a leader, another a counselor, and another an administrator or helper, and we need each to do God's work. Therefore, believers are interdependent. To neglect the church by not using our gifts or relying on the gifts of others is to disable the church and to, also, spiritually impoverish ourselves. We need the eyes—the insight of others—and we need the ears—someone who will listen to us and care—and they need us as well. (2) The body metaphor also teaches us how Christ gets his work done on the earth. The church is Christ's hands, feet, mouth, eyes, and ears. We may be the only Christ others will see, hear, or touch. Through us, his message is told, the weak are encouraged, the sick are healed, the lost are saved, and his justice is manifested.

Are we participating in Christ's body and therefore his work of building up believers and saving an unbelieving world?

4. The church is pictured as a family.

In Matthew 12:49-50, Christ said this as he pointed to his disciples: "Here are my mother and my brothers. For whoever does the will of my Father in heaven is my brother and sister and mother." By saying this in the context of his mother and brothers asking for him (v. 47), Christ elevated spiritual family, even over natural family at times.

This reality shows us at least two things about the church. (1) It teaches that we should treat members of the church as family. In 1 Timothy 5:1-2, Paul said: "Do not address an older man harshly but appeal to him as a father. Speak to younger men as brothers, older women as mothers, and younger women as sisters—with complete purity." In fact, in Paul's letters, he commonly used family terminology to address the church and its members—calling them brothers (or brothers and sisters, depending on the Bible translation used). (2) In addition, the family metaphor reminds believers that they should prioritize the church over other people and things. In Galatians 6:10, Paul said, "So then, whenever we have an opportunity, let us do good to all people, and especially to those who belong to the family of faith." Believers should do good to all, but especially to other believers. This, no doubt, includes prioritizing gathering together to worship, fellowship, and serve. Hebrews 10:24-25 says:

> And let us take thought of how to spur one another on to love and good works, not abandoning our own meetings, as some are in the habit of doing, but encouraging each other, and even more so because you see the day drawing near.

With spiritual family, we should continually think about them, love them, and meet together for mutual edification.

5. The church is pictured as a soldier.

In Ephesians 6:10-12, Paul said:

Finally, be strengthened in the Lord and in the strength of his power. Clothe yourselves with the full armor of God so that you may be able to stand against the schemes of the devil. For our struggle is not against flesh and blood, but against the rulers, against the powers, against the world rulers of this darkness, against the spiritual forces of evil in the heavens.

Then in verses 13-18, he describes the spiritual armor believers must wear such as the breastplate of righteousness, the belt of truth, the shield of faith, the sword of God's Word, etc. These primarily refer to godly character traits and disciplines, which enable us to stand in our spiritual war against the devil and his demons. This means one of God's purposes for the church is to be combative—defeating the devil and his work in individuals, society, and the world.

Christ mentioned this in Matthew 16:18, when describing his plan to build the church. He said, "… on this rock I will build my church, and the gates of Hades will not overpower it." This is not a defensive picture but an offensive picture. It's a picture of the church moving forward against the kingdom of Satan and the gates eventually falling. This happens as believers share the gospel and unbelievers come to Christ. It happens as unrighteous practices in communities and government are exposed and destroyed, as races are reconciled, unborn babies are delivered from abortion, trafficking is abolished, and justice happens in courts. Since the church represents Christ, it should expose evil and seek to bring righteousness in all areas. Ultimately, Christ will bring perfect righteousness when he comes to judge sin and rule the earth with his saints.

6.   The church is pictured as a temple.

In 1 Corinthians 3:16-17, Paul says: "Do you not know that you are God's temple and that God's Spirit lives in you? If someone destroys God's temple, God will destroy him. For God's temple is holy, which is what you are." When Paul says, "Do you not know that you are God's temple," the "you" is plural. Paul was referring to the church as God's temple. Likewise, in 1 Peter 2:5, Peter said, "you yourselves, as living stones, are built up as a spiritual house to be a holy priesthood and to offer spiritual sacrifices that are acceptable to God through Jesus Christ."

What does this mean practically about the church's purpose? (1) It means the church is a place where God meets with believers. In Matthew 18:20, Christ said, "For where two or three are assembled in my name, I am there among them." Though given in the context of church discipline, Christ is present any time people gather in his name to worship and serve him (cf. Ps 34:7, 1 Cor 3:16). (2) In addition, the church's ultimate focus, before serving one another or others, is to worship God. Hebrews 13:15-16 says:

Through him then let us continually offer up a sacrifice of praise to God, that is, the fruit of our lips, acknowledging his name. And do not neglect to do good and to share what you have, for God is pleased with such sacrifices.

The writer of Hebrews, in using the metaphor of sacrifices offered at the temple in worship, said that the believers' praise, acts of goodness, and generosity are spiritual sacrifices that please God. Being a temple reminds us that the church's focus is meeting with the living God and worshiping him. In fact, Romans 12:1 says that we should offer our bodies—referring to every part of our lives—as living sacrifices to God.

7. The church is pictured as a workmanship or masterpiece.

In Ephesians 2:10, Paul says, "For we are his workmanship, having been created in Christ Jesus for good works that God prepared beforehand so we may do them." (1). Being called "God's workmanship" demonstrates how the church was created for good works. This is true both individually and corporately, as the letter was written to local churches in Asia Minor and the individuals in those churches. As individuals, God has given us various gifts, talents, and experiences to use in building his kingdom. But, this is also true of local churches. Not all churches are the same. Some are especially gifted in missions, others deep teaching, others caring for the poor (possibly because of the community they are in), and others charismatic gifts. This reminds us that we not only need other believers as Christ's body but also other churches. The body of Christ is not the local church, as though each could function independent of others; the body is the church universal, consisting of many congregations, which need each other to do the works God has called us to. (2) Also, "workmanship" can be translated "masterpiece" (NLT). This seems to demonstrate the beauty of God's church and how perfectly he made her. This reminds us that the church is meant to bring glory to God, as it builds up believers and serves its communities. Matthew 5:16 says, "In the same way, let your light shine before people, so that they can see your good deeds and give honor to your Father in heaven."

8. The church is pictured as a bride.

Ephesians 5:25-26 and 31-32 says:

> Husbands, love your wives, just as Christ loved the church and gave himself for her to sanctify her by cleansing her with the washing of the water by the word … For this reason a man will leave his father and mother and will be joined to his wife, and the two will become one flesh. This mystery is great—but I am actually speaking with reference to Christ and the church.

Paul taught that the marriage between a husband and wife is really meant to picture how Christ loves the church, his bride. The church being a bride teaches us several things about the church: (1) It demonstrates God's everlasting commitment to her. Marriages today may end because of the fault of one or both mates. However, God's love for his bride, as flawed as she may be, will never end. Romans 8:35-39 says,

> Who will separate us from the love of Christ? Will trouble, or distress, or persecution, or famine, or nakedness, or danger, or sword? As it is written, "For your sake we encounter death all day long; we were considered as sheep to be slaughtered." No, in all these things we have complete victory through him who loved us! For I am convinced that neither death, nor life, nor angels, nor heavenly rulers, nor things that are present, nor things to come, nor powers, nor height, nor depth, nor anything else in creation will be able to separate us from the love of God in Christ Jesus our Lord.

God's unfailing love and commitment remind us of the eternal security of every true believer (cf. John 10:27-30). God is committed to his church eternally and the individuals who are part of her—not one of them will ever be lost (cf. John 6:37-39). (2) Also, the church as a bride pictures how the church should submit to Christ, even as the Christian wife should her husband as the leader of their home (cf. Eph 5:22-23). One of the identifying characteristics of true believers is doing the will of God. In Matthew 7:21, Christ said this: "Not everyone who says to me, 'Lord, Lord,' will enter the kingdom of heaven, but only the one who does the will of my Father who is in heaven." (3) Finally, the bride as a wife reminds us that the church is a co-heir and ruler with Christ. Romans 8:17 says, "And if children, then heirs (namely, heirs of God and also fellow heirs with Christ)—if indeed we suffer with him so we may also be glorified with him." When Christ returns, the church will rule the heavens and earth with Christ, as his bride (cf. Rev 19:7-8).

Reflection

1. What metaphor stood out most and why?
2. Why does God give us metaphors of the church?
3. What other metaphors does Scripture use for the church or believers specifically (cf. John 15:1-11, etc.)?
4. What other questions or applications did you take from the reading?

Church Government

What type of government should the church have? Who are its leaders? It is clear in Scripture that Christ is the head of the church. According to Ephesians 1:22, after Christ was raised from the dead and seated at the right hand of the Father, "God put all things under Christ's feet, and he gave him to the church as head over all things." Christ is the head of the church; however, he leads his church through delegated leaders called elders and deacons. The elders provide oversight, teaching, and care, and deacons support the elders by caring for the manual needs of the congregation. In the early church, it seems that every church had a plurality of elders, as the term is almost always mentioned in the plural (Acts 14:23, 15:2, 20:17; Titus 1:5; Jam 5:14). Typically, the only exceptions are when an elder is being singled out or the qualifications of an elder are being given (1 Tim 5:19, Titus 1:6, etc.). With deacons, as mentioned, they were the servants of the church—focusing on manual tasks, such as finances and administration and caring for the congregation. They support the elders so they can focus on their primary ministry of prayer and the Word (cf. Acts 6:2-4). Some believe that though every church must have elders, each one does not necessarily have to have deacons. In Titus, Paul calls him to set up elders in Crete and gives qualifications of elders, but never calls him to set up deacons (Titus 1). Because of this, it seems like deacons are selected on an as-needed basis to support the needs of the church (cf. Acts 6:1-6).

Though the elders are the leaders of the church and the congregation is called to follow their lead (Heb 13:7, 17), the congregation should participate in many of the major decisions. For example, this is clearly seen when the apostles commissioned the church to select seven men (often considered the first deacons or the precursor to deacons) who would care for the widows in Acts 6:1-6. Then, the apostles confirmed the congregation's choices by laying hands on these men. Also, it is seen in how the Jerusalem church participated in the decision of the apostles and the elders to send leaders to the church of Antioch with letters. Acts 15:22 says:

> Then the apostles and elders, with the whole church, decided to send men chosen from among them, Judas called Barsabbas and Silas, leaders among the brothers, to Antioch with Paul and Barnabas.

Further support for the congregation participating in some major decisions with the elders is seen in Christ's teaching on church discipline. In Matthew 18:17, the final step before excommunication is that the unrepentant member's situation is brought before the church, and not specifically the elders. It says: "If he refuses to listen to them, tell it to the church. If he refuses to listen to the church, treat him like a Gentile or a tax collector."

Therefore, church government is supposed to be a combination of elder-rule and congregational participation in some of the major decisions. Certainly, everything shouldn't be brought before the church, as it would take forever for anything to get done. However, certain major decisions, as discerned by the elders, such as buying property, confirming the annual budget, selecting deacons or other leadership positions, and removing an unrepentant member from membership should include the congregation in the process. And as a wisdom principle for following this form of church government, Wayne Grudem said, "Government works best when it has the consent of those governed."[9] Sometimes this form of church government is called elder-led congregationalism.

In the following sections, we will take a more intimate look at elders and deacons, including their qualifications.

Reflection

1. What stood out most in the reading and why?
2. What are biblical supports for elder-led congregationalism?
3. What are other forms of church government?
4. What form of government is used in your church or church background?
5. What other questions or applications did you take from the reading?

Elders

There are several names used for the primary leaders of the church. In 1 Timothy 3:1-2, they are called "overseers," some versions translate this as "bishops." We see in other places including 1 Timothy 5:17, they are called elders. In 1 Peter 5:2, they are called shepherds or pastors.

In some denominations, these are three separate positions: pastors are over the elders, and bishops are over the pastors. However, in Scripture, these are different names for the same position. (1) Evidence for this is the fact that Paul only lists two leadership positions (overseers and deacons) when teaching Timothy about how the church should be run in 1 Timothy 3:1-15. (2) Also, Acts 20:17, 28-30 and 1 Peter 5:1-2 use the titles elders, bishops, and pastors (shepherds), interchangeably. For example, 1 Peter 5:1-2 says:

> So as your fellow elder and a witness of Christ's sufferings and as one who shares in the glory that will be revealed, I urge the elders among you: Give a shepherd's care to God's flock among you, exercising oversight not merely as a duty but willingly under God's direction, not for shameful profit but eagerly

Likewise, in Titus 1:5-7, the term elder and bishop are used interchangeably.

Why does Scripture give three different titles for the same position? The different titles focus on the different qualities of the office:

- Elder refers to the spiritual maturity and wisdom of these leaders.
- Pastor is a shepherding term referring to their care for others.
- Bishop refers to their oversight or rulership of the church.

Qualities of Elders

What are qualities of elders? In 1 Timothy 3:1-7, Paul wrote this:

This saying is trustworthy: "If someone aspires to the office of overseer, he desires a good work." The overseer then must be above reproach, the husband of one wife, temperate, self-controlled, respectable, hospitable, an able teacher, not a drunkard, not violent, but gentle, not contentious, free from the love of money. He must manage his own household well and keep his children in control without losing his dignity. But if someone does not know how to manage his own household, how will he care for the church of God? He must not be a recent convert or he may become arrogant and fall into the punishment that the devil will exact. And he must be well thought of by those outside the faith, so that he may not fall into disgrace and be caught by the devil's trap.

1. They must desire to be overseers or pastors (v. 1). He says, "if someone aspires to the office of overseer." God is looking for willing leaders. Again, in 1 Peter 5:2, Peter said

this to elders about their attitude in serving, "not merely as a duty but willingly."

2. Their inward call must be affirmed by the outward call of the church. The fact that the qualities of elders are given to Timothy implies that the church's leaders (and possibly the entire congregation) need to affirm these qualities in potential elders. In fact, in Titus 1:5, Paul told Titus to "appoint elders in every town" (Titus 1:6-9).

3. The qualifications are primarily character traits. They must not be "violent," which literally means "not a giver of blows"[10] (v. 3). They must manage their own household well (v. 4). They must be given to "hospitality," which means "to love strangers"[11] (v. 3). Elders are to be examples of godly character within a church. In fact, in 1 Peter 5:3, Peter directly called for the elders to "be examples to the flock."

4. The only skill needed is that they must be "an able teacher" (v. 2). Since they must be able to teach, it means they must know the Word of God and be competent in explaining it to others. This skill in teaching may include preaching from the pulpit, but not necessarily. The most effective teaching is one-on-one or in small groups.

5. They must be men.

• The requirement of male leadership is clear from Paul's use of male pronouns throughout the passage.

Again 1 Timothy 3:2-7 says,

> The overseer then must be above reproach, the husband of one wife, temperate, self-controlled, respectable, hospitable, an able teacher, not a drunkard, not violent, but gentle, not contentious, free from the love of money. He must manage his own household well and keep his children in control without losing his dignity. But if someone does not know how to manage his own household, how will he care for the church of God? He must not be a recent convert or he may become arrogant and fall into the punishment that the devil will exact. And he must be well thought of by those outside the faith, so that he may not fall into disgrace and be caught by the devil's trap.

- The requirement of male leadership is also taught in other Pauline passages.

Titus 1:6 says, "An elder must be blameless, the husband of one wife, with faithful children who cannot be charged with dissipation or rebellion." First Timothy 2:12-13 says, "I do not allow a woman to teach or exercise authority over a man. She must remain quiet. For Adam was formed first and then Eve." Similarly, 1 Corinthians 14:34 says, "women should be silent in the churches, for they are not permitted to speak. Rather, let them be in submission, as in fact the law says."

The traditional view that only males can serve in pastoral leadership is called the complementarian view. This view recognizes that males and females are equally made in the image of God and given gifts by God. However, in the home and in the church, God has given the two sexes different roles. Males are called to lead in both the home and the church (cf. Eph 5:25-27, Titus 1:6). This view comes primarily from taking the previously mentioned texts at face value.

Egalitarian View

The view that women can serve in church leadership (and for some also lead the home) is called the egalitarian view. This view would say that God has made both males and females in God's image and there are no differing roles.

What supports are used for the egalitarian position, specifically for women serving as pastors in churches?

1. Egalitarians support their position by teaching that the verses calling for women to not teach males or pastor in the church were referring to specific situations in those churches or that culture and therefore should not be universally applied to churches today.

Complementarians would point out that the context of those verses and the repetition of Paul's teaching in different contexts argue for his teaching being universal. For example, in 1 Timothy 2:12-13, when Paul says, "I do not allow a woman to teach or exercise authority over a man. She must remain quiet. For Adam was formed first and then Eve," he does not make an argument unique to the Ephesian church or to that culture. He makes a creation argument—"For Adam was formed first and then Eve." Paul argues that God's creation of Eve after Adam demonstrates his leadership over her. Adam's leadership is also demonstrated in the fact that he named his wife (Gen 2:23, 3:20), just like he previously named the animals at God's prompting (Gen 2:19-20). Furthermore, in 1 Corinthians 14:33-34 (NET), when Paul gave instructions for women to practice restraint in their speaking in churches, he said: "… As in all the churches of the saints, the women should be silent in the churches, for they are not permitted to speak. Rather, let them be in submission, as in fact the law says." Paul's teaching in 1 Corinthians was not only for Corinth but for "all the churches of the saints" (v. 33). In addition, he pointed to the law as evidence. He probably referred either to the same creation argument used in 1 Timothy 2:13 or to the fact that only men were allowed to be priests in the Old Testament. Essentially, Paul said, God made it this way from the beginning—both in marriage and in the tabernacle/temple.

2. Egalitarians support their position by stating that gender roles have been abolished in Christ.

They would use verses like Galatians 3:28-29, which says, "There is neither Jew nor Greek, there is slave nor free, there is neither male nor female —for you are all one in Christ Jesus. And if you belong to Christ, then you are Abraham's descendants, heirs according to the promise." Complementarians would argue against this since the context of the verse is Paul arguing about our equal standing in Christ, not our various roles. If male and female roles in the home and church were abolished, this would also be true of slaves and free (which in those times was often equivalent to an employee and employer), yet Paul teaches slaves to submit to their masters and women to submit to their husbands in other writings (Eph 5:23, 6:5, Col 3:18, 22). People can be equal in Christ and have differing roles, even as people in the work force are equal in worth and yet commonly have different roles.

3. Egalitarians support their position by emphasizing examples in Scripture of potential women in leadership.

For example, Romans 16:7 says, "Greet Andronicus and Junia, my compatriots and my fellow prisoners. They are well known to the apostles, and they were in Christ before me." Junia was a common female name during that time. Therefore, taking this text into consideration alone, it is possible that she was an apostle. Some might point to the women at the tomb when Christ resurrected. They were sent out to declare to the apostles that Christ had resurrected (Matt 28:7). It's often said, "Those women were preachers!" In addition, Deborah, who was a prophet and judge of Israel (Jdg 4-5), is used as an argument for women serving in pastoral leadership.

How do complementarians handle those arguments? (1) They would typically first state that none of those women, necessarily, served in positions forbidden in the New Testament. They were not pastors in the church. In fact, Paul even spoke about women prophesying in 1 Corinthians 11:5 and so did Luke in Acts 21:9. Also, it's possible that Paul spoke about Phoebe as a deaconess in Romans 16:1, though not a pastor. The ministries that those women served in don't necessarily conflict with Paul's teaching that women could not serve as pastor/elders. Women are called to serve, make disciples, preach the gospel, and lead in some circumstances, as all believers are. The question is, "What is the proper context of their serving?" (2) With Junia being "well known to the apostles," the text is ambiguous—meaning it's not clear whether she was an apostle or "well-known" by the apostles. As far as being an apostle like the Twelve, it seems clear that she wasn't one of those. In Acts 1:21, when selecting a replacement for Judas, Peter declared that the next apostle had to be a male. He said, "Thus one of the men who have accompanied us during all the time the Lord Jesus associated with us, beginning from his baptism by John until the day he was taken up from us—one of these must become a witness of his resurrection together with us." With that said, the word "apostle" simply means "sent one," and therefore could be used in a general sense to refer to those commissioned and sent by churches to serve, like missionaries today (cf. 2 Cor 8:23; Phil 2:25, "messenger"). If Junia was an apostle, the text could be referring to her as a missionary—not somebody who numbered with the Twelve. (3) With Deborah specifically, not only was she not equivalent to a pastor of a church, but also the book of Judges is not meant to be prescriptive of how things should be. The book shows how disobedient Israel was, including their leaders. Each judge in the book seems to get worse, finishing with the worst judge, Samson. He was the leader of Israel, but he married a woman from Israel's enemy, the Philistines. He was a drunk who continually entertained prostitutes, which eventually led to his death. With Deborah's narrative, the focus seems to be on how there was no male leadership in Israel. In Judges 4:9, she said to Barak, "I will indeed go with you. But you will not gain fame on the expedition you are undertaking, for the Lord will turn Sisera over to a woman." Deborah's narrative, like most narratives in Judges, shows how bad Israel had gotten. It doesn't show what should be normative for the people of God in that era or the current one. In fact, in Isaiah 3:12, Isaiah describes God's judgment over Israel in this way: "Youths oppress my people, women rule over them" (cf. 3:1-7).

4. Some egalitarians support their position because of a liberal view of Scripture.

For them, instead of seeing Scripture as without error in all that it teaches and to be the believers' rule of life in all areas, they often question Scripture's teachings and reject it on certain points. Commonly, they would reject a literal interpretation of Scripture and take a more spiritual or figurative interpretation. For example, they might accept what the Bible teaches about salvation by faith alone, but reject what it says about sexuality, homosexuality, male leadership, creation, miracles, and/or the resurrection, and take a more figurative view of those doctrines. Some might even reject the idea of Christ being the only way to salvation. They might be considered very similar to the Sadducees in Christ's day. The Sadducees, though believing in the Jewish God and studying Scripture, often rejected a literal interpretation of Scripture. This led to not believing in angels, demons, miracles, or even the resurrection. Likewise, some accept women as pastors because of a liberal understanding of Scripture, which commonly rejects literal interpretations of certain verses and doctrines.

Complementarian View

What are the typical supports for the complementarian view—that only men can serve as pastors?

1. As mentioned, complementarians base their view on taking the New Testament verses which teach women should not serve as pastors at face value.

First Timothy 3:1 says, "… If someone aspires to the office of overseer, 'he' desires a good work." Titus 1:6 says, "An elder must be blameless, the 'husband' of but one wife, with faithful children who cannot be charged with dissipation or rebellion." First Timothy 2:12-13 says, "I do not allow a woman to teach or exercise authority over a man. She must remain quiet. For Adam was formed first and then Eve." Similarly, 1 Corinthians 14:34 says, "women should be silent in the churches, for they are not permitted to speak. Rather, let them be in submission, as in fact the law says."

2. Complementarians base their view on the continuity of male leadership from the Old Testament.

As mentioned, in 1 Timothy 2:12-13, Paul taught that women should not teach males in the church based on the fact that "Adam was formed first, then Eve." He refers to the order of creation, arguing that God made Adam as Eve's leader. Also, in 1 Corinthians 14:34, when Paul taught that women should practice restraint in their speaking while in the church, he argued that this submission was taught in the Law—the Old Testament. He says, "the women should be silent in the churches, for they are not permitted to speak. Rather, let them be in submission, as in fact the law says." Again, this could possibly refer to the order of creation argument, as in 1 Timothy 2:12-13. But he also might be referring to the leaders—priests and Levites—in the tabernacle and temple who were required to be male (cf. Ex 29:29-30).

3. Complementarians base their view on males and females being made in God's image and symbolizing the equality, submission, and perfect love in the Trinity.

In 1 Corinthians 11:3, Paul says, "But I want you to know that Christ is the head of every man, and the man is the head of a woman, and God is the head of Christ." Since males and females are made in the image of God, they demonstrate aspects of God's triune nature. In the Trinity, God the Father and God the Son are co-equal, but in their relationship, there is headship—the Son submits to the Father. In a marriage, Paul compares the woman to Christ and the husband to God the Father—the husband is the head of the wife just as God is the head of Christ (1 Cor 11:3). The husband and wife are co-equal, but there is headship in their relationship, as they are made in the image of God. This headship is also seen in the male leadership of the church. In the church, males and females are equal; however, all the members are called to submit to the designated male leadership in the church (cf. Heb 13:17). This equality and submission reflect the dynamics in the Trinity.

It should also be added that there is perfect love in the Trinity (1 John 4:8), and because of that, perfect love should be demonstrated in the home and church dynamics, along with submission and authority. These are true throughout society since people are made in God's image. When love, submission, and authority break down, relationships and society in general break down.

The Elders' Duties

What are the elders' duties? There are many:

1. They should rule or oversee the affairs of the church (1 Tim 5:17).
2. They should focus on prayer and the ministry of God's Word (cf. Acts 6:4).
3. They should be servants (1 Pt 5:2).
4. They should be godly examples for the flock (1 Pt 5:3).
5. They should train members to do the work of ministry (Eph 4:11-12).
6. They should help members mature from spiritual infancy to spiritual maturity by teaching them Scripture (Eph 4:14).
7. They should pray for the sick (Jam 5:14-15).
8. They should set church policy (Acts 15:22).
9. They should ordain other men (Acts 14:23, Titus 1:5, 1 Tim 4:14).
10. They should protect the church from false teaching (Acts 20:28-31).

Reflection

1. What stood out most in the reading and why?
2. Who are elders and what do they do?
3. What are the qualities of elders?
4. How should elders be selected?
5. Can women serve in the pastoral role? Why or why not? Support your position with Scripture.
6. What other questions or applications did you take from the reading?

Deacons

The word "deacon" means "servant." It was used of those who waited on tables serving food and did menial work.[12] Deacons are the servants of the church. Their ministry seems to have begun in Acts 6:3-4 when the apostles sought men "full of the Spirit and of wisdom" who would serve the widows in the church. This allowed the apostles to focus on prayer and ministry of the Word (Acts 6:4). It seems that deacons fulfill a similar role, supporting the work of elders in the church.

First Timothy 3:8-12 gives the requirements for deacons:

Deacons likewise must be dignified, not two-faced, not given to excessive drinking, not greedy for gain, holding to the mystery of the faith with a clear conscience. And these also must be tested first and then let them serve as deacons if they are found blameless. Likewise also their wives must be dignified, not slanderous, temperate, faithful in every respect. Deacons must be husbands of one wife and good managers of their children and their own households.

Like the requirements for elders, deacons must have godly character. The primary difference between the requirements of an elder and a deacon in Chapter 3 is the fact that an elder is "an able teacher" (v. 2). As the title "deacon" or "servant" suggests, they focus on the manual aspects of the church, like finances and administration, so that the elders can focus on ruling, preaching, and prayer (cf. Acts 6:4, Heb 13:17). With that said, though their primary role isn't teaching, they must know God's Word and practice it faithfully. First Timothy 3:9 says they should be "holding to the mystery of the faith with a clear conscience."

There is some debate over whether 1 Timothy 3:11 allows women to serve as deacons in the church. The NET and other versions say, "In the same way, their wives are to be women worthy of respect." However, since "wives" in the Greek can be translated as "women," some interpret the verse as giving requirements for deaconesses instead of the deacon's wives (cf. NIV, NASB, etc.).

What are evidences for translating the word as "women," instead of "wives," allowing for female deacons?

1. The addition of the word "likewise" (v. 11) seems to be introducing and distinguishing a separate group from the elders and deacons. [13] Paul also introduced and distinguished the deacons from the elders with the word "likewise" (v. 8).

2. "There is no possessive pronoun or definite article connecting these women with deacons."[14] The possessive pronoun "their," in some translations, is supplied by the translators for understanding.

3. There is no requirement given for the elders' wives in the previous verses (1 Tim 3:1-7). Why would there be requirements for the deacons' wives and not the elders'?

4. There seems to be biblical evidence for women deacons in the NT. In Romans 16:1, Phoebe is given the title of "servant" or "deacon."

5. Since the deacons' ministry is not primarily ruling and teaching, which Paul taught was reserved for qualified

males (1 Tim 2:12, 3:1-7), there seems to be no biblical reason for women to be disqualified from the position.

Therefore, many believe that deacons can be both males and females who have godly character, know God's Word, and have a heart to serve.

Reflection

1. What stood out most in the reading and why?
2. Who are deacons and what are their roles in the church?
3. Can women serve as deacons? Why or why not?
4. What other questions or applications did you take from the reading?

Church Ordinances

What are the ordinances or sacraments which the church should regularly practice as a part of worship? Generally speaking, an ordinance is any type of rule or regulation set up by an authority.[15] The church has two ordinances which were set by Christ: baptism and the Lord's Supper (Lk 22:19-20, Matt 28:19). In some denominations, ordinances are called sacraments because they are sacred and a means by which God gives grace to church members. Since sacraments are at times considered a means of grace for achieving salvation, such as in Catholicism, others prefer the term ordinance, because they were ordained by Christ and are a symbolic reminder of foundational doctrines.[16] In the following sections, we will consider both baptism and the Lord's Supper, including various views on them.

Baptism

What is baptism? Acts 2:41 says, "So those who accepted his message were baptized, and that day about three thousand people were added." The people in Jerusalem heard the preaching of Peter and 3,000 repented and accepted Christ as their Lord and Savior. Immediately, they were baptized and added to the number of the church. Baptism in the early church was the first step of obedience after salvation. They accepted Christ and immediately were baptized. This is an ordinance, a command, we are called to follow as believers in Christ. In Matthew 28:19-20, Jesus said this to his disciples:

> Therefore go and make disciples of all nations, baptizing them in the name of the Father and of the Son and of the Holy Spirit, teaching them to obey everything I have commanded you. And remember, I am with you always, to the end of the age.

Charles Ryrie said this about baptism:

> Theologically, baptism may be defined as an act of association or identification with someone, some group, some message, or some event. Baptism into the Greek mystery religions associated the initiates with that religion. Jewish proselyte baptism associated the proselyte with Judaism. John the Baptist's baptism associated His

followers with His message of righteousness (he had no group for them to join). (Incidentally, John was apparently the first person ever to baptize other people—usually baptisms were self-administered.) For James and John to be baptized with Christ's baptism meant to be associated with His suffering (Mark 10:38–39). To be baptized with the Spirit associates one with the body of Christ (1 Cor. 12:13) and with the new life in Christ (Rom. 6:1–10). To be baptized into Moses involved identification with his leadership in bringing the Israelites out of Egypt (1 Cor. 10:2). ... Christian baptism means identification with the message of the Gospel, the person of the Savior, and the group of believers.[17]

Infant Baptism and Believer's Baptism

Now it should be noted that throughout history there have been two primary camps on baptism. There is "believer's baptism" or "credobaptism." "Credo" comes from the Latin word for creed or belief. Those in this camp believe that only those who repent and make a conscious decision to follow Christ can be baptized. However, the second view is "infant baptism" or "pedobaptism." "Pedo" comes from the Greek word for children. Those who hold this view would baptize adults who recently accepted Christ, but they would also baptize the infants of believers.

Infant Baptism

What supports are used for infant baptism? Two primary supports are used:

1. Pedobaptists argue that infant baptism demonstrates God's covenant with not only believers but their children.

It is argued that Abraham's children and Israel's children were circumcised before having their own faith (Gen 17:10-12). Since circumcision was a sign of the covenant with God in the Old Testament and baptism is a sign of the covenant in the New, children of believers should be baptized. In Colossians 2:11-12, circumcision and baptism seem to correspond with one another.

> In him you also were circumcised—not, however, with a circumcision performed by human hands, but by the removal of the fleshly body, that is, through the circumcision done by Christ. Having been buried with him in baptism, you also have been raised with him through your faith in the power of God who raised him from the dead.

Likewise, Peter said this in Acts 2:38-39,

> Repent, and each one of you be baptized in the name of Jesus Christ for the forgiveness of your sins, and you will receive the gift of the Holy Spirit. For the promise is for you and your children, and for all who are far away, as many as the Lord our God will call to himself.

Charles Ryrie's summary of this common argument is helpful:

> The argument rests on the covenant theology concept of a single covenant of grace that involved an initiatory rite into that covenant, the rite being circumcision in the Old Testament and baptism in the New. These rites indicate membership in the covenant, not necessarily personal faith.[18]

2. Pedobaptists point to the "household" passages in Acts of whole families getting baptized.

For example, in Acts 16, Lydia's household was baptized, and the jailer's family was baptized as well. Consider the passages:

> A woman named Lydia, a dealer in purple cloth from the city of Thyatira, a God-fearing woman, listened to us. The Lord opened her heart to respond to what Paul was saying. After she and her household were baptized, she urged us, "If you consider me to be a believer in the Lord, come and stay in my house." And she persuaded us.
> Acts 16:14-15

> They replied, "Believe in the Lord Jesus and you will be saved, you and your household." Then they spoke the word of the Lord to him, along with all those who were in his house. At that hour of the night he took them and washed their wounds; then he and all his family were baptized right away.
> Acts 16:31-33

They would argue that there were probably infants in the house, who were baptized.

Believer's Baptism

What are the arguments for practicing believer's baptism and not infant baptism?

1. Credobaptists point to the fact that baptism is always commanded after belief (or repentance)—not before.

Acts 2:38 says, "Peter said to them, 'Repent, and each one of you be baptized in the name of Jesus Christ for the forgiveness of your sins, and you will receive the gift of the Holy Spirit.'" Matthew 28:19 says, "Therefore go and make disciples of all nations, baptizing them in the name of the Father and the Son and the Holy Spirit."

2. Credobaptists point out that only believers are baptized in the New Testament.

There is never a command in Scripture to baptize infants or an example of it. In the "household" texts that pedobaptists sometimes refer to, an infant is never mentioned. For example, Acts 16:33 says, "At that hour of the night he took them and washed their wounds; then he and all his family were baptized right away." It is best to assume that not only did the jailer accept Christ, but so did his family. In Acts 16:31, Paul and Silas told the jailer that he and his family should believe in Christ: "Believe in the Lord Jesus and you will be saved, you and your household." Since the family was baptized, apparently, they also believed.

Reflection

1. What stood out most in the reading and why?
2. What are supports for infant baptism?
3. What are supports for believer's baptism?
4. Which form of baptism (infant or believer's) do you think is most biblical and why?
5. How and when were you baptized?
6. How should churches handle believers who desire membership but have different views on baptism or were baptized in a different tradition (infant or believer's baptism)?

7. What other questions or applications did you take from the reading?

Mode of Baptism

As we look at church history, there have been several modes of baptism. A mode is a manner or way something is done. The primary modes of baptism have been sprinkling, immersion, and pouring.

What are some brief reasons why churches and denominations use these differing modes?

The Case for Sprinkling

There are several reasons commonly used to support sprinkling:

1. There were certain Old Testament ordinances that required sprinkling that symbolized their cleansing, and these sprinklings are once called "baptisms" in Hebrews 9:10.

For example, Leviticus 14:7 says, "and sprinkle it seven times on the one being cleansed from the disease, pronounce him clean, and send the live bird away over the open countryside." Exodus 24:8 says, "So Moses took the blood and splashed it on the people and said, 'This is the blood of the covenant that the Lord has made with you in accordance with all these words.'" Likewise, as mentioned, in Hebrews 9:10 the Greek word for baptism is used to describe these Old Testament sprinklings—called "washings" in the text. It says, "They served only for matters of food and drink and various washings; they are external regulations imposed until the new order came."

2. Sprinkling symbolizes the cleansing we experience from God in the New Covenant.

   Ezekiel 36:25-27 says,

   I will sprinkle you with pure water and you will be clean from all your impurities. I will purify you from all your idols. I will give you a new heart, and I will put a new spirit within you. I will remove the heart of stone from your body and give you a heart of flesh. I will put my Spirit within you; I will take the initiative and you will obey my statutes and carefully observe my regulations.

3. There are times when immersion is improbable, as in places where water is sparse such as a desert. This also may be true when someone is deathly sick.

4. Historically, the majority of churches have baptized through sprinkling.[19]

The Case for Immersion

What are supports for immersion?

1. The Greek word "baptizo" used of baptism naturally means to plunge, dip, or immerse something.[20] It was used of a cloth being put in die to change the color. The whole cloth would have to be immersed.

2. The fact that the baptisms in Scripture occurred in large bodies of water, such as with Christ and Philip, supports immersion.

Matthew 3:16 says, "After Jesus was baptized, just as he was coming up out of the water, the heavens opened and he saw the Spirit of God descending like a dove and coming on him." It is very clear that Jesus went into a body of water to be baptized. That's why it says, "he was coming up out of the water."

Also, we see this with Philip and the Ethiopian in Acts 8:38-39. It says,

> So he ordered the chariot to stop, and both Philip and the eunuch went down into the water, and Philip baptized him. Now when they came up out of the water, the Spirit of the Lord snatched Philip away, and the eunuch did not see him any more, but went on his way rejoicing.

Here we see the words "down into" and "up out of." The immersionist would ask the question, "Why go down into a body of water just to sprinkle or pour water on somebody?" The use of large bodies of water and the terminology of going "down" and coming "up" strongly suggest immersion.

3. Immersion seems to best symbolize our baptism into Christ's body and his death and resurrection.

First Corinthians 12:13 states that we have been baptized with the Spirit into Christ and have become his body. It says, "For in one Spirit we were all baptized into one body. Whether Jews or Greeks or slaves or free, we were all made to drink of the one Spirit."

Also, in Scripture, the word "baptism" is used of the believer's death and resurrection with Christ. Romans 6:4 says, "Therefore we have been buried with him through baptism into death, in order that just as Christ was raised from the dead through the glory of the Father, so we too may live a new life."

Immersionists would argue only full immersion could picture us becoming fully immersed into Christ's body and our death and resurrection with him.

4. Historically, Gentile converts to Judaism were immersed. They stripped naked and then dipped themselves fully into a tank of water. Practicing immersion would seem to naturally follow as Gentiles became part of Christ's church in the New Covenant.[21]

The Case for Pouring

What are supports for pouring, the least practiced view of the three?

1. It is argued that pouring best pictures the Holy Spirit coming onto the life of a believer. For example, Joel 2:28-29 (which is repeated in Acts 2:17-18), says,

    After all of this, I will pour out my Spirit on all kinds of people. Your sons and daughters will prophesy. Your elderly will have revelatory dreams; your young men will see prophetic visions. Even on male and female servants I will pour out my Spirit in those days.

2. There is evidence that this was practiced at times in ancient history. There are ancient drawings in catacombs of people being waist deep in water with a person pouring water onto them.[22]

Why is there so much diversity in the church over the mode of baptism? Undoubtedly, the reason for such diversity is because

Scripture never clearly commands an exact procedure for baptism—how much water and how it should be done. Why? We can be sure that what is most important to God, he is very clear on. He is very clear about salvation through faith alone and the need for repentance. But in this area, he is not as clear. What is clear is that believers should be baptized as soon as possible after salvation (Acts 2:38).

If God wanted to be clear about the amount of water, he could have been. Consider the great details God gave for Old Testament ordinances, such as the procedures for the grain and drink offerings in Numbers 15:4-5:

> then the one who presents his offering to the Lord must bring a grain offering of one-tenth of an ephah of finely ground flour mixed with one fourth of a hin of olive oil. You must also prepare one-fourth of a hin of wine for a drink offering with the burnt offering or the sacrifice for each lamb.

There had to be 1/10 of an ephah of flour, 1/4 of a hin of oil, and 1/4 of a hin of wine. If God wanted to be specific in the amount of water and the procedure of baptism, he could have been, as with other ordinances in the Old Testament. This is why there has been considerable diversity on the mode of baptism throughout history. For this reason, it is wise for Christians to not be divisive over the mode of baptism.

Reflection

1. What stood out most in the reading and why?
2. What are the three modes for baptism and some evidences for them?
3. Which mode do you think is most biblical and why?

4. What other questions or applications did you take from the reading?

75

Is Baptism Necessary for Salvation?

Whether baptism is necessary for salvation is an important question to ask, since there are some verses that at least seem to indicate that it is. For example, Acts 2:38 says, "Peter said to them, 'Repent, and each one of you be baptized in the name of Jesus Christ for the forgiveness of your sins, and you will receive the gift of the Holy Spirit.'" Also, Mark 16:16 says, "The one who believes and is baptized will be saved, but the one who does not believe will be condemned." The belief that baptism is necessary for salvation is called baptismal regeneration.

With both verses, after closer inspection, it is clear that neither teaches baptismal regeneration. In the case of Acts 2:38, when it says, "be baptized in the name of Jesus Christ for the forgiveness of your sins," the word "for" would be better translated "because of."[23] Believers should be baptized in the name of Jesus Christ because their sins have been forgiven. Also, in Mark 16:16, it says, "the one who believes and is baptized will be saved," but then says, "the one who does not believe will be condemned." A person is condemned for not believing. It says nothing about being condemned because of not being baptized. This text should not be pressed to say what it does not say. The New Testament knows nothing of an unbaptized Christian, and therefore the text speaks generally about a baptized believer. It is not meant to deal with an unusual situation in which one believes and is not baptized.

With all that said, as with any verse, we must compare it to what the rest of Scripture teaches on the subject. In the case of baptism and salvation, the Bible is clear that salvation is by grace through faith alone in Jesus Christ—not by works (Eph 2:8-9, John 3:16, Rom 10:9-10). So, any interpretation which comes to the conclusion that baptism, or any other act, is necessary for salvation, is a faulty interpretation.

Ephesians 2:8-9 says, "For by grace you are saved through faith, and this is not from yourselves, it is the gift of God; it is not from works, so that no one can boast." If baptism was a work necessary for salvation, then people would have something to boast about. But because salvation is of faith, and even our faith is a gift according to this passage (cf. Phil 1:29), all praise and glory go to God.

What are other evidences that baptism is not salvific?

The Argument of the Thief on the Cross & Cornelius the Centurion

One of the stronger arguments is the salvation of the thief on the cross who was never baptized and the story of Cornelius the centurion who received the Holy Spirit before baptism. Luke 23:42 describes the conversation between the thief and Christ: "Then he said, 'Jesus, remember me when you come in your kingdom.' And Jesus said to him, 'I tell you the truth, today you will be with me in paradise.'" Jesus declared that the thief would be in paradise, and obviously, he would not have a chance to be baptized before it. His salvation was based on faith alone. Similarly, we see that Cornelius in Acts 10 received the Holy Spirit before baptism, which means that he was saved. Acts 10:44-48 says,

> While Peter was still speaking these words, the Holy Spirit fell on all those who heard the message. The circumcised believers who had accompanied Peter were greatly astonished that the gift of the Holy Spirit had been poured out even on the Gentiles, for they heard them speaking in

tongues and praising God. Then Peter said, "No one can withhold the water for these people to be baptized, who have received the Holy Spirit just as we did, can he?" So he gave orders to have them baptized in the name of Jesus Christ.

The Argument of Paul and Jesus

In addition, if baptism is necessary for salvation, then it would seem strange for Paul to boast about not baptizing people and to declare Christ "did not send" him to "baptize." In 1 Corinthians 1:14-17, he said:

> I thank God that I did not baptize any of you except Crispus and Gaius, so that no one can say that you were baptized in my name! (I also baptized the household of Stephanus. Otherwise, I do not remember whether I baptized anyone else.) For Christ did not send me to baptize, but to preach the gospel—and not with clever speech, so that the cross of Christ would not become useless.

These comments would not make any sense if baptism was necessary for salvation.

Furthermore, according to the Gospels, Christ never baptized people. John 4:1-2 says, "Now when Jesus knew that the Pharisees had heard that he was winning and baptizing more disciples than John (although Jesus himself was not baptizing, but his disciples were)." If salvation came through baptism, it would make sense to see Christ baptizing people. However, he didn't.

Baptism is an important step of obedience after salvation; but, it is not salvific. Salvation is a gift of God, not based on our works. It happens by grace through faith (cf. Eph 2:8-9, Rom 10:13).

Reflection

1. What stood out most in the reading and why?
2. What verses are commonly used to support the necessity of baptism for salvation?
3. What are arguments against baptismal regeneration?
4. What other questions or applications did you take from the reading?

The Lord's Supper

For I received from the Lord what I also passed on to you, that the Lord Jesus on the night in which he was betrayed took bread, and after he had given thanks he broke it and said, "This is my body, which is for you. Do this in remembrance of me." In the same way, he also took the cup after supper, saying, "This cup is the new covenant in my blood. Do this, every time you drink it, in remembrance of me." For every time you eat this bread and drink the cup, you proclaim the Lord's death until he comes.
1 Corinthians 11:23-26

Christ gave the Lord's Supper as an ordinance or sacrament for believers to continually practice. The fact that Christ said, "Do this in remembrance of me," means that celebrating the supper is not optional (1 Cor 11:24). Unlike baptism which should only happen once in a believer's life, the Lord's Supper should be routinely practiced by believers as a perpetual memorial of Christ's death (1 Cor 11:26). To not practice it or to neglect it is sin.[24] The supper was commonly taken as part of a meal or love feast in the early church (Jude 12, 1 Cor 11:20-21). We'll consider the significance of the Lord's Supper, the views of it, and the requirements for taking it.

Significance

What is the significance of the Lord's Supper?

1. It is an act of fellowship and intimacy with God.

In the same way that eating with someone is an act of fellowship and intimacy, so is taking the Lord's Supper. In the Old Testament, there were various instances and opportunities to eat in the presence of God. For example, after God made a covenant with Israel in Exodus, Moses and seventy elders went up Mount Sinai, beheld God, and ate before him. Exodus 24:9-11 says:

> Moses and Aaron, Nadab and Abihu, and the seventy elders of Israel went up, and they saw the God of Israel. Under his feet there was something like a pavement made of sapphire, clear like the sky itself. But he did not lay a hand on the leaders of the Israelites, so they saw God, and they ate and they drank.

In addition, there were ceremonies instituted in Israel, as part of God's law, where the offeror would eat in the presence of God at the tabernacle and later the temple, such as with the giving of the tithe and the fellowship offering. Deuteronomy 14:23 and 26 says this about the tithe:

> In the presence of the Lord your God you must eat from the tithe of your grain, your new wine, your olive oil, and the firstborn of your herds and flocks in the place he chooses to locate his name, so that you may learn to revere the Lord your God always... Then you may spend the money however you wish for cattle, sheep, wine, beer, or whatever you desire. You and your household may eat there in the presence of the Lord your God and enjoy it.

Leviticus 19:5-6 says this about the fellowship offerings:

When you sacrifice a peace offering sacrifice to the Lord, you must sacrifice it so that it is accepted for you. It must be eaten on the day of your sacrifice and on the following day, but what is left over until the third day must be burned up.

Similarly, in the New Covenant, though we don't offer sacrifices or eat our tithes before the Lord, God has given us the Lord's Supper as a fellowship meal that we eat in his presence. In Luke 22:19, the Supper was something Christ ate with his disciples, and as we eat it, the Lord is, no doubt, present with us as Scripture promises (cf. 1 Cor 3:16). In Matthew 18:20, Christ said this: "For where two or three are assembled in my name, I am there among them."

2. It is an act of unity and fellowship among believers.

In 1 Corinthians 10:17, Paul says, "Because there is one bread, we who are many are one body, for we all share the one bread." The bread represents Christ's body which was broken for believers, but the bread also represents the unity of believers, since believers are Christ's body (Col 1:18). Therefore, the Lord's Supper is a fellowship meal amongst believers.

3. It is a proclamation of the New Covenant and our participation in its benefits.

Luke 22:20 says, "And in the same way he took the cup after they had eaten, saying, 'This cup that is poured out for you is the new covenant in my blood." The word covenant means "to cut." Typically, when people made covenants with one another in ancient times, they would kill an animal to declare the solemnness of their agreement and their need to fulfill the requirements of it. Similarly, Christ made a covenant with us through his blood. He covenanted to forgive our sins, fill us with his Spirit, write his laws on our hearts, and empower us to obey them (cf. Ez 31:31-34, 36:26-27). Our covenant was initiated and cut through the body of Christ on the cross, fulfilled by him, and now we are in a covenant relationship with him.

4. It is a remembering of Christ's death.

First Corinthians 11:26 says, "For every time you eat this bread and drink the cup, you proclaim the Lord's death until he comes." Taking of the elements is like a memorial, where we frequently remember Christ's death for our sins. This is important, because we're so prone to forget the great cost of our salvation and its benefits.

5. It is an act of faith declaring that God has forgiven us and that we will not bear his wrath for our sins.

Whon Christ ate the Last Supper with his disciples before his death, it was also a celebration of the Jewish Passover meal; however, Christ imbued it with rich new meaning. At Israel's original Passover, they were slaves in Egypt and were instructed to put the blood of a lamb over their doorposts, so their first born would not be killed by God when he passed over Egypt. The New Testament teaches that the original Passover lambs always foreshadowed Christ. In 1 Corinthians 5:7, Paul said, "For Christ, our Passover lamb, has been sacrificed." Therefore, in the Lord's Supper, we are declaring by faith that we will not bear God's wrath, because our Lamb already died for us and his blood protects us.

6. It is a looking forward to Christ's second coming.

Again 1 Corinthians 11:26 says, "For every time you eat this bread and drink the cup, you proclaim the Lord's death until he comes." In the Lord's Supper, believers not only look back at Christ's death but look forward to his return. This is important because we are so prone to become consumed with life as it is and not be zealous for the coming of Christ. When we take the supper, we declare with other believers, "Come, Lord Jesus!" (Rev 22:20).

7. It looks forward to the time we will eat with God and other believers in heaven.

Wayne Grudem said it this way:

Yet even the Lord's Supper looks forward to a more wonderful fellowship meal in God's presence in the future, when the fellowship of Eden will be restored and there will be even greater joy, because those who eat in God's presence will be forgiven sinners now confirmed in righteousness, never able to sin again. That future time of great rejoicing and eating in the presence of God is hinted at by Jesus when he says, "I tell you I shall not drink again of this fruit of the vine until that day when I drink it new with you in my Father's kingdom" (Matt. 26:29). We are told more explicitly in Revelation about the marriage supper of the Lamb: "And the angel said to me, 'Write this: Blessed are those who are invited to the marriage supper of the Lamb'" (Rev. 19:9). This will be a time of great rejoicing in the presence of the Lord, as well as a time of reverence and awe before him.[25]

8. It is an act of intimacy with Christ.

In 1 Corinthians 10:16, Paul said, "Is not the cup of blessing that we bless a sharing in the blood of Christ? Is not the bread that we break a sharing in the body of Christ?" The way in which we participate in Christ's blood and body has created much controversy amongst believers. The points of contention are, "In what ways do believers participate in Christ's body while taking the Lord's Supper?" and "What does Christ mean by 'this is my body' in Luke 22:19?" We'll consider these:

Views

There are four main views about what it means to participate in the body of Christ in the Lord's Supper:

1. The Catholics believe in transubstantiation, or the actual presence view.[26]

The word "transubstantiation" derives from Latin—"trans" means "change" and "substantiation" means "substance"; therefore, in the supper, there is a "change of substance." The term is used to show how the bread and wine are physically changed into the body and blood of Christ when the priest declares, "This is my body" during the celebration of mass.[27] Also, Roman Catholics believe that every time the Lord's Supper is celebrated, in some way, Christ's sacrifice literally happens again—Christ dies for the sins of the world.

The problem with this view is it fails to recognize the symbolic nature of Christ's words, "This is my body" (Lk 22:19). When the disciples were eating the supper, they would not have viewed the bread as actually becoming Christ's body, since Christ was standing in front of them. And the breaking of the bread was symbolic, as well. Christ did not die in front of them; the breaking of the bread foreshadowed his death. Likewise, when Christ said, "This cup that is poured out for you is the new covenant in my blood" in Luke 22:20, it meant that the cup and the juice being poured out symbolized the initiation of the New Covenant through Christ's shed blood. It wasn't literally the New Covenant. The

Catholic view fails to recognize the symbolic nature of the elements.

In addition, the Catholic view fails to recognize the finality of Christ's sacrifice. There is no need for it to happen over and over again, every time the supper is taken. In Hebrews 10:1-3, the author states that the Old Testament sacrifices were offered yearly because they could not make the worshipers perfect; therefore, every year the sacrifices were a reminder of sin. However, he contrasts those sacrifices with Christ's sacrifice which only needed to happen once. Hebrews 10:12 says, "But when this priest had offered one sacrifice for sins for all time, he sat down at the right hand of God." Christ sat down because his work, as far as paying for the sins of the world, was finished for all time.

2. The Lutherans believe in consubstantiation, or the real presence view.[28]

Even though Luther rejected the Catholic view of the elements becoming the body of Christ, he believed Christ was still physically present in the Lord's Supper. He believed that the presence of Christ existed in the elements (the bread and juice), without becoming them. Luther illustrated this by the analogy of an iron in fire; the iron becomes red-hot, but both the iron and the fire individually remain the same.[29] Also, he used the illustration of water in a sponge. Water saturates the sponge, but individually, they remain the same.

Like the Catholic view, the Lutheran view fails to recognize the symbolic language of "This is my body" (Lk 22:19). If we pressed the symbolism, we could use the same hermeneutic with "This cup that is poured out for you is the new covenant in my blood" (Luke 22:20).

3. Reformers commonly believe in the spiritual presence view of Christ in the Lord's Supper.

Calvin rejected the physical presence views of the Catholics and the Lutherans. He believed the supper was indeed symbolic but more than symbolic. When people eat of the elements, "they do contain his spiritual body and blood."[30] Calvin said it this way:

> Yes, Christ's human body is locally present in heaven, but—Calvin said—it doesn't have to descend in order for believers to truly partake of it. Why? Because the Holy Spirit makes true fellowship possible here and now. The Holy Spirit is Christ's Spirit. He lifts us to the heavenlies to feed on Christ. Those who eat the bread and drink the wine in faith are also, by the power of the Holy Spirit, actually being nourished by the body and blood of Christ.[31]

4.   The other prominent view is the memorial or symbolic view.

Since Christ said, "Do this in remembrance of me" (Lk 22:19b), Zwingli, another protestant reformer, believed that the supper was primarily symbolic—meant to be a memorial of Christ's death. Those who hold this view do not deny that Christ is spiritually present when participating in the supper, but Christ is spiritually present only in the sense that he is always present with believers and that he is especially present when believers gather in his name. In Matthew 28:20, Christ said, "And remember, I am with you always, to the end of the age." And, in Matthew 18:20, he said, "For where two or three are assembled in my name, I am there among them." Christ does not become the elements or enter the elements (physically or spiritually), but he is present spiritually as we worship and serve him. This is the most common understanding of the Lord's Supper in the protestant church today.

Requirements

There are two requirements for taking the Lord's Supper—though some would argue for more.

1. Salvation: Since the Lord's Supper includes participation in the New Covenant, we must have experienced it. We must be born again. Again, Luke 22:20 says, "And in the same way he took the cup after they had eaten, saying, 'This cup that is poured out for you is the new covenant in my blood.'" Some advocate for an open table where nonbelievers can participate. However, in 1 Corinthians 11:28-31, which we will consider in the next point, Paul warns about the need for self-examination, lest we eat and drink judgment upon ourselves. An unbeliever who participates in the elements without repenting of sin would only endanger himself, even as an unrepentant Christian would.

2. Self-examination: Since Christ died to deliver us from the power and penalty of sin, we must confess known sins as we partake in it, instead of holding onto them. In 1 Corinthians 11, believers were disciplined for taking the supper unworthily—meaning they were practicing unrepentant sin.

    First Corinthians 11:28-31 says,

    A person should examine himself first, and in this way let him eat the bread and drink of the cup. For the one who eats and drinks without careful regard for the body eats and drinks judgment against himself. That is why many of you are weak and sick, and quite a few are dead. But if we examined ourselves, we would not be judged.

Those who were living in unrepentant sin while taking the supper brought judgment on themselves. In the context, the unrepentant sins were living selfishly, practicing drunkenness, and causing division. While participating in the Lord's Supper, the poor Corinthian believers were being neglected and left out, while the rich were eating and getting drunk (1 Cor 11:20-22). Because of this, God disciplined the believers. Some had become depressed, others sick, and some had even died because they had disrespected the Lord's Supper. To live in unrepentant sin and to take the supper, which symbolizes Christ's death for our sins, is to dishonor Christ and bring judgment on ourselves.

3. Some believe one must be baptized before participating in the Lord's Supper.

There is no clear Scripture which teaches this; however, to be unbaptized for some might represent rebellion toward God's clearly revealed will. In 1 Corinthians 11:28-29, Paul taught that believers should examine themselves before taking part in the supper—meaning repenting of sin. As mentioned, if we participate in the supper while continuing in sin, it might lead to God disciplining us. Therefore, in that sense, it might be wise for a believer who is unwilling to be baptized to not participate in the supper. However, if they are unbaptized because there has not yet been an opportunity at their church, then that doesn't seem to be a good reason to not obey Christ's command to remember his sacrifice by participating in the supper (1 Cor 11:24-25).

4. Some believe one must not be under church discipline to take the Lord's Supper.

Those who hold this view take it from Paul's writing on church discipline in 1 Corinthians 5:11-13. He says:

But now I am writing to you not to associate with anyone who calls himself a Christian who is sexually immoral, or greedy, or an idolater, or verbally abusive, or a drunkard, or a swindler. Do not even eat with such a person. For what do I have to do with judging those outside? Are you not to judge those inside? But God will judge those outside. Remove the evil person from among you."

In verse 11, when it says "do not even eat" with a believer walking in rebellion, many believe this refers to the Lord's Supper. The church was to expel this unrepentant sinner, and therefore, they would be barred from the Lord's Supper. However, "do not even eat" is ambiguous. It probably refers to not fellowshipping with an unrepentant believer altogether, as to help him see the seriousness of his sin. In Matthew 18:15-17, Christ gives the process of church discipline, and the last step, after repeated attempts to help the person repent of some sin, the unrepentant believer should be treated like a tax collector or sinner—meaning to separate from him, in order to help him repent (Matt 18:17). Therefore, when Paul says to not eat with an unrepentant believer, he is not referring to the Lord's Supper specifically but to not fellowshipping with the person in general, which would include not eating the Lord's Supper with them.

Reflection

1. What stood out most in the reading and why?
2. What does the Lord's Supper signify for the believer?
3. What are the four views of the Lord's Supper? Which do you believe is most biblical?
4. What are the requirements for taking the Lord's Supper?

5. How have you experienced special grace while taking the Lord's Supper?
6. Should believers practice the Lord's Supper only at church or can it be practiced in small groups and with families (cf. Acts 2:42-47)?
7. What other questions or applications did you take from the reading?

Church Membership

Do we need to join a local church? Is formal church membership something the Bible teaches? Some don't think so, including some churches and denominations. It is commonly argued, "God knows who are his. All believers are part of the universal church. The Bible never explicitly commands formal church membership. Why then should joining a specific church be encouraged or required?" Certainly, salvation is most important, and the New Testament never explicitly commands formal church membership. However, formal membership in a local church is clearly implied throughout the New Testament and is, therefore, expected of every believer.

How does the Bible demonstrate the need for formal church membership?

1. Evidence for church membership is seen in the fact that many of the New Testament epistles were written to local churches or their leaders (Colossians, Philippians, 1 and 2 Timothy, etc.).

Obviously, when those letters were received, people had to be able to distinguish whether they were part of those churches or not. Likewise, in Revelation 2-3, Christ actually gave commendations and/or rebukes to seven local churches. To Christ, there were specific people identified with those local congregations whom those words applied to and people outside of them whom the words did not apply. Without a formal membership, how could those believers and their leaders know who were part of those churches?

2. Evidence for church membership is seen in the language in Acts about the early church.

For instance, Acts 2:41 says this about the church in Jerusalem: "So those who accepted his message were baptized, and that day about three thousand people were added." When people had repented and were baptized, they were added to the existing believers—the church. It is clear that the church was keeping a numerical count of those added to them. Acts 4:4 says that number grew to 5,000. Therefore, they were keeping track of who were part of the church.

Also, many other statements in Acts point to a well-defined church membership. Acts 8:1 refers to the "church in Jerusalem." Acts 15:22 talks about a gathering and decision by "the whole church," again describing the Jerusalem church. In order for the "whole church" to be gathered and agree on something, there must be a distinguishable and well-defined group. Likewise, Acts 14:23 recounts Paul and Barnabas appointing elders in "various churches." The language in Acts of the early church argues for a defined membership.

3. Evidence for church membership is the fact that elders are called to shepherd local churches and will be held accountable for doing so.

In Hebrews 13:17, the author said this to Jewish Christians, "Obey your leaders and submit to them, for they keep watch over your souls and will give an account for their work." If elders are going to give an account to God for the members of their flock, they must know who belongs to it. They are not accountable for every church visitor or person who attends church. They are accountable for those who have publicly committed to the church and its leadership.

4. Evidence for church membership is Christ's command to practice church discipline.

In Matthew 18:15-18, Christ gave a four-step process for restoring a sinning member. This includes going to them one on one, with another person (or two), then bringing it before the church, and finally the person being removed from fellowship (Matt 5:18; cf. 1 Cor 5:11). Logically, only somebody who is clearly part of a local church and submitted to her leadership can be removed from church fellowship.

5. Evidence for church membership is the need for believers to fulfill the "one another" texts in the New Testament.

For example, Hebrews 10:24-25 says:

And let us take thought of how to spur one another on to love and good works, not abandoning our own meetings, as some are in the habit of doing, but encouraging each other, and even more so because you see the day drawing near.

Instead of forsaking the assembly, we are called to faithfully meet together, to "spur one another on to love and good works" and "encourage each other," as we wait for Christ's coming. Also, 1 Peter 4:10 says: "Just as each one has received a gift, use it to serve one another as good stewards of the varied grace of God." We are each called to find our gifts and use them to "serve one another." It is hard to faithfully do these without committing to and regularly meeting with a local body of believers.

Though Scripture never explicitly commands joining a local church, it is clearly implied throughout the New Testament and, therefore, expected. In joining a local congregation, we commit to pray for those believers, to serve them, to hold them accountable, to help them grow, and to partner in reaching the lost locally and globally, among other things.

The Mission of the Church

What is the mission of the church? According to Scripture, the church has three primary missions.

The Church's Mission Is to Worship God

The chief mission God has given the church is to praise and worship him. In 1 Peter 2:9, Peter said this to the church, "But you are a chosen race, a royal priesthood, a holy nation, a people of his own, so that you may proclaim the virtues of the one who called you out of darkness into his marvelous light." In a world that is dark and ignores or denies God (Rom 1:21), the church is called to corporately praise his name and pray for others to do so. In the Lord's Prayer, Christ taught believers to pray, "Hallowed be your name" (Matt 6:9 NIV). It is a petition for God to be worshiped throughout the earth.

God calling the church out of the world to worship him is very similar to God calling Israel to worship him, when most nations worshiped pagan deities. Through Moses, God said this to Pharaoh who had enslaved the Israelites, "Let my people go, so that they may worship me in the wilderness" (Ex 7:16 NIV).

In fact, in heaven, the angels and believers from all periods of history eternally worship God. Revelation 5:11-13 describes this:

> Then I looked and heard the voice of many angels in a circle around the throne, as well as the living creatures and

the elders. Their number was ten thousand times ten thousand—thousands times thousands—all of whom were singing in a loud voice: "Worthy is the lamb who was killed to receive power and wealth and wisdom and might and honor and glory and praise!" Then I heard every creature—in heaven, on earth, under the earth, in the sea, and all that is in them—singing: "To the one seated on the throne and to the Lamb be praise, honor, glory, and ruling power forever and ever!"

When churches gather to worship throughout the week, it foreshadows what will happen throughout eternity. The church worships as it sings psalms and hymns to the Lord (Eph 5:19), reads, proclaims, and obeys God's Word (1 Tim 4:13, Jam 1:22), participates in the ordinances of baptism and the Lord's Supper (Matt 28:19, 1 Cor 11:24-26), gives of its best to the Lord (2 Cor 9:7), and serves one another (Gal 6:10, Jam 1:27).

Characteristics of True Worship

In John 4:23-24, Christ gave general requirements for worship when speaking to the woman at the well, which should be observed both individually and corporately, as the church gathers for worship. He said:

But a time is coming—and now is here—when the true worshipers will worship the Father in spirit and truth, for the Father seeks such people to be his worshipers. God is spirit, and the people who worship him must worship in spirit and truth.

Worship that God accepts must be in spirit and in truth. There is some argument over whether "spirit" refers to the Holy Spirit or the human spirit. They are both true. Christian worship should be inspired and empowered by God's Spirit. In Ephesians 5:18-20, Paul described one of the fruits of being filled and empowered by God's Spirit as worship. He said,

> And do not get drunk with wine, which is debauchery, but be filled by the Spirit, speaking to one another in psalms, hymns, and spiritual songs, singing and making music in your hearts to the Lord, always giving thanks to God the Father for each other in the name of our Lord Jesus Christ,

When the Spirit is really ruling in our lives, it leads us to worship—both corporately (speaking to one another in psalms, hymns, and spiritual songs) and individually (making music in your hearts to the Lord).

With that said, when Christ says true worshipers will worship the Father in spirit and truth, "spirit" probably refers to the human spirit.[32] Typically, when referring to the Holy Spirit, an "article" is used to distinguish it from the human spirit or demonic spirits. John 4:23-24 lacks that article; therefore, Christ is distinguishing true worship from false worship by focusing on our hearts. Likewise, in 1 Corinthians 13:1-3, Paul described various types of worship which were displeasing to God because they lacked love—the right heart. He said:

> If I speak in the tongues of men and of angels, but I do not have love, I am a noisy gong or a clanging cymbal. And if I have prophecy, and know all mysteries and all knowledge, and if I have all faith so that I can remove mountains, but do not have love, I am nothing. If I give away everything I own, and if I give over my body in order to boast, but do not have love, I receive no benefit.

Also, the author of Hebrews said this: "Now without faith it is impossible to please him, for the one who approaches God must believe that he exists and that he rewards those who seek him" (Heb 11:6). If, as believers, we worship God apart from faith by doubting or not trusting God, it is not acceptable to him.

Furthermore, if we worship God while holding onto unrepentant sin, it hinders our worship as well. In Psalm 66:18, the Psalmist said, "If I had harbored sin in my heart, the Lord would not have listened." First Timothy 2:8 says, "So I want the men to pray in every place, lifting up holy hands without anger or dispute." Matthew 5:8 says, "Blessed are the pure in heart, for they will see God."

Christ lamented this lack of a right spirit—a right heart—in the Pharisees' worship. In Matthew 15:8-9, he said, "This people honors me with their lips, but their heart is far from me, and they worship me in vain, teaching as doctrines the commandments of men." True worship approaches God with a right heart—a heart of love, faith, and purity.

In addition, Christ taught that true worship must be in "truth" (John 4:23-24). This means that we can't worship God in any way we choose, even if we have right hearts. In the Old Testament, God gave meticulous details to Israel about how to approach him in worship. It included requirements for the types of offerings, clothing for the priests, specific dates, etc. Though we are in the New Covenant, God still gives requirements for worship according to his Word. For example, in public worship, Scripture calls us to read the Bible (1 Tim 4:13), preach the Bible (2 Tim 4:2), sing the Bible (Eph 5:19, Col 3:16), to pray according to the Bible (1 Tim 2:1-3), and to practice the sacraments, which symbolize the truths of God's Word (Matt 28:19, 1 Cor 11:23-26). Everything in public worship must align with Scripture—with God's truth.

For the reformers in the Great Reformation, they called this the regulative principle. In Catholic worship, which the reformers protested against, there were many elements not supported by Scripture—such as worshipping Mary, praying to saints, the belief in purgatory, and penance. These acts of worship failed the regulative principle—they did not agree with God's Word. Likewise, the public worship of the church must teach God's Word, align with it, and not contradict it. This applies to the singing of songs. Are they biblical? Do they teach truth? This applies to the preaching. Is the Word of God being proclaimed or the preacher's life, politics, or sports? This applies to church traditions and customs. They must all align with the truth of God's revealed Word.

In the same way God delivered Israel out of Egypt to worship him in the wilderness, God has called the church out of the world to worship him. We are to worship him not only in corporate gatherings, but in everything we do. In 1 Corinthians 10:31, Paul said, "So whether you eat or drink, or whatever you do, do everything for the glory of God." Acceptable worship to God must be in spirit—aiming to love him with all of our hearts, approaching him in faith and in purity—and worship must be in truth—according to Scripture.

The Church's Mission Is to Equip Believers

Another one of the primary missions God has given the church is to equip believers to grow and do God's work. Ephesians 4:11-14 describes God's plan for this:

> It was he who gave some as apostles, some as prophets, some as evangelists, and some as pastors and teachers, to equip the saints for the work of ministry, that is, to build up the body of Christ, until we all attain to the unity of the faith and of the knowledge of the Son of God— a mature person, attaining to the measure of Christ's full stature. So we are no longer to be children, tossed back and forth by waves and carried about by every wind of teaching by the trickery of people who craftily carry out their deceitful schemes.

God specifically gave gifted leaders, including pastors and teachers, to teach believers doctrine, to train them to serve, to help bring unity in the church, to protect them, and to help believers look more like Christ. Paul describes immature believers as spiritual children (4:11). As with little children who are prone to danger because of a lack of knowledge, wisdom, and experience, spiritual children are prone to the deception of false teaching (4:14), discord (1 Cor 3:1-3), idolatry (1 Cor 3:4), and even spiritual pride (1 Tim 3:6), which all lead to further sin (1 Tim 1:19) and, for some, even falling away from God (Heb 6:4-6). Therefore, one of the primary missions of the church is to spiritually equip believers to know Christ, be like him, and serve like him. This is done through the means of grace God gives the church—the preaching of God's Word, reading it, singing it, and praying it, practicing the sacraments of baptism and the Lord's Supper, fellowshipping with the saints, serving, and practicing church discipline, among other things. In Colossians 1:28-29, Paul succinctly summarizes this mission:

> We proclaim him by instructing and teaching all people with all wisdom so that we may present every person mature in Christ. Toward this goal I also labor, struggling according to his power that powerfully works in me.

Maturing and equipping believers must be the church's goal today as well.

Church Discipline

As mentioned, church discipline is one of the ways believers are equipped for the work of ministry. The goal of church discipline is to restore a sinning brother, warn other believers who might be compromising in sin or tempted to compromise (1 Tim 5:20), and therefore maintain the purity and witness of the church before God and the world (Eph 5:27, cf. 1 Tim 3:7). In Matthew 18:15-20, Christ describes the process of church discipline:

> "If your brother sins, go and show him his fault when the two of you are alone. If he listens to you, you have regained your brother. But if he does not listen, take one or two others with you, so that at the testimony of two or three witnesses every matter may be established. If he refuses to listen to them, tell it to the church. If he refuses to listen to the church, treat him like a Gentile or a tax collector. "I tell you the truth, whatever you bind on earth will have been bound in heaven, and whatever you release on earth will have been released in heaven. Again, I tell you the truth, if two of you on earth agree about whatever you ask, my Father in heaven will do it for you. For where two or three are assembled in my name, I am there among them."

In Christ's four-step church discipline process, (1) the sinning believer should first be approached one on one (Matt 18:15). This means people should not gossip about this person or spread rumors; he should be approached privately. This is especially important because there could be some misunderstanding, and even if the person is in sin, gossiping about him may unnecessarily close his heart to rebuke. If an unrepentant person repents when approached privately, then the discipline process ends. (2) If the sinning believer does not repent, then two or three people should confront him (Matt 18:16). The hope is that because of increased pressure, the erring person may recognize the seriousness of his sin and repent. In addition, the extra person (or persons) provides witnesses if there is no repentance. (3) If the sinning believer still will not repent, his situation should be brought before the church (Matt 18:17). Practically, this implies that this person's situation is probably brought before the elders, and then the elders will carefully investigate before bringing it before the congregation. This sin is brought publicly before the congregation, in part, so that the congregation is warned and reminded of the seriousness of sin. In 1 Timothy 5:20, Paul said this about an unrepentant elder: "Those guilty of sin must be rebuked before all, as a warning to the rest." But, the erring person's sin is primarily brought before the church so that they can reach out to that erring member in hopes of repentance (1 Tim 1:20, 1 Cor 5:5). (4) If the sinning believer still does not repent, the church members should exclude him from church fellowship, including not eating or fellowshipping with him (Matt 18:17, 2 Thess 3:6, 11-15). In 1 Corinthians 5:11-13, Paul said this in the context of church discipline:

> But now I am writing to you not to associate with anyone who calls himself a Christian who is sexually immoral, or greedy, or an idolater, or verbally abusive, or a drunkard, or a swindler. Do not even eat with such a person. For what do I have to do with judging those outside? Are you not to judge those inside? But God will judge those outside. Remove the evil person from among you.

Being excluded from the fellowship of the church is not a punishment but a continuing attempt to help this person repent by returning to God and his people (1 Tim 1:20, 1 Cor 5:5). This loving accountability aims to not only protect the individual from sin and its consequences but also the church. In 1 Corinthians 5:6, Paul said: "Your boasting is not good. Don't you know that a little yeast affects the whole batch of dough?" In using yeast as a metaphor for sin and a batch of dough for the church, Paul was saying that sin left unchecked will spread throughout the church. Therefore, church discipline is a form of accountability from church members to preserve the holiness and the witness of the church (Heb 12:15, 1 Cor 6:6, Eph 5:27, 1 Tim 3:7).

Not all sins require church discipline, since no one in the church is perfect. It would be hard to discipline somebody for pride or unforgiveness, though those sins should certainly be addressed. However, overt, unrepentant sins such as sexual immorality, idolatry, false teaching, divisiveness, verbal abuse, drunkenness, theft, and the like, as mentioned by Paul in various places (1 Cor 5:11, Titus 1:10-11, 3:8-11), must be disciplined. Wayne Grudem's comments on the sins disciplined by churches in the New Testament are helpful:

> all sins that were explicitly disciplined in the New Testament were publicly known or outwardly evident sins, and many of them had continued over a period of time. The fact that the sins were publicly known meant that reproach was being brought on the church, Christ was being dishonored, and there was a real possibility that others would be encouraged to follow the wrongful patterns of life that were being publicly tolerated.[33]

After giving instructions on church discipline in Matthew 18, Christ says, "I tell you the truth, whatever you bind on earth will have been bound in heaven, and whatever you release on earth will have been released in heaven" (v. 18). His words simply mean that when the church disciplines in accordance with Christ's instructions, they have God's authoritative approval. As John MacArthur aptly said: "Church discipline is therefore an earthly expression of heaven's holiness."[34]

Along with studying God's Word, prayer, corporate worship, the Lord's Supper, fellowship, and other means of grace, church discipline also equips the saints to do the work of ministry as it protects them from sin (and Satan), which can destroy the witness and fruitfulness of individual believers and the church as a whole.

The Church's Mission Is to Minister to Unbelievers

There are two primary ways in which the church ministers to unbelievers and that is through evangelism and mercy ministries. [35] In Matthew 28:19-20, Christ gave the great commission to his disciples when he said:

> Therefore go and make disciples of all nations, baptizing them in the name of the Father and of the Son and of the Holy Spirit, teaching them to obey everything I have commanded you. And remember, I am with you always, to the end of the age."

Believers should pray for the lost (1 Tim 2:1-3) and share the gospel with them (1 Cor 15:1-4, 2 Tim 4:5)—the message that all people are sinners under the wrath of a righteous God, that Christ died to pay the penalty of their sins and rose again from the dead, and that people must repent of their sins and believe in Christ as their Lord and Savior to be saved (Rom 3:23, 6:23, 10:9-10). With that said, the great commission is not simply to make converts, but disciples. This includes baptizing new believers, connecting them with a Bible-preaching church, and training them there.

However, though the church's primary hope for unbelievers is that they become disciples of Christ, believers should demonstrate God's love and care to them, even if they reject Christ. When Christ was on the earth, he not only shared the good news with the lost but fed the hungry, healed the sick, and healed the demonically oppressed, among other things. He cared for both their spiritual and physical needs. Believers should do the same, as they seek to reflect Christ. In Luke 6:35-36, Christ said:

> But love your enemies, and do good, and lend, expecting nothing back. Then your reward will be great, and you will

be sons of the Most High, because he is kind to ungrateful and evil people. Be merciful, just as your Father is merciful.

We are to be merciful, like God, even to those who reject him. In James 1:27, James said, "Pure and undefiled religion before God the Father is this: to care for orphans and widows in their misfortune and to keep oneself unstained by the world." Widows and orphans were the poorest and most commonly taken advantage of people in society, and God expects believers to love and care for them—no doubt, as a bridge for them to ultimately accept Christ, if they haven't already.

Sometimes the church argues over whether Christians should focus on mercy ministries and social justice at all, as though it might minimize the priority of spreading the gospel; however, it is very clear from Scripture that God wants believers to both share the gospel and care for the temporal needs of a hurting world, even as Christ did. Certainly, the gospel must be the priority, as we practically show God's love to a broken and needy world. Wayne Grudem's comments on this are helpful:

Such ministries of mercy to the world may also include participation in civic activities or attempting to influence governmental policies to make them more consistent with biblical moral principles. In areas where there is systematic injustice manifested in the treatment of the poor and/or ethnic or religious minorities, the church should also pray and—as it has opportunity—speak against such injustice. All of these are ways in which the church can supplement its evangelistic ministry to the world and indeed adorn the gospel that it professes. But such ministries of mercy to the world should never become a substitute for genuine evangelism or for the other areas of ministry to God and to believers mentioned above.[36]

The mission of the church is to worship God, equip believers, and minister to unbelievers by sharing the gospel with them and serving them.

Reflection

1. What stood out most and why?
2. What are the three missions of the church?
3. How does the church accomplish the mission of worshipping God?
4. How does the church accomplish the mission of equipping believers?
5. How does the church accomplish the mission of ministering to unbelievers?
6. Why has there at times been controversy over the church's ministry of evangelizing unbelievers and showing mercy to them? Why are they commonly pitted against one another?
7. What other questions or applications did you take from the reading?

Conclusion

Before Christ died and resurrected, he promised to build his church (Matt 16:18). The church is the followers of Christ. It includes Jews and Gentiles who have repented of their sins and put their faith in Christ, as Lord and Savior. It is local, regional, and universal. It is visible, including true followers and false ones, and invisible, including the redeemed in heaven and on earth. It is both an organism, as the body of Christ who does his work on earth, and an organization, including leadership, such as elders and deacons. The church is also missional in that it is called to worship God, equip believers, and minister to unbelievers by seeking their eternal good. May God continue to empower his church to be his hands and feet to the glory of his name!

Study Group Tips

Leading a small group using the Bible Teacher's Guide can be done in various ways. One format for leading a small group is the "study group" model, where each member prepares and shares in the teaching. This appendix will cover tips for facilitating a weekly study group.

1. Each week the members of the study group will read through a selected chapter of the guide, answer the reflection questions (see Appendix 2), and come prepared to share with the group.

2. Prior to each meeting, a different member can be chosen to lead the group and share Question 1 of the reflection questions, which is to give a short summary of the chapter read. This section of the gathering could last from five to fifteen minutes. This way, each member can develop their gift of teaching. It also will make them study harder during the week. Or, each week the same person could share the summary.

3. After the summary has been given, the leader for that week will facilitate discussions through the rest of the reflection questions and also ask select review questions from the chapter.

4. After discussion, the group will share prayer requests and pray for one another.

The strength of the study group is the fact that the members will be required to prepare their responses before the meeting, which will allow for easier discussion. In addition, each member will be given the opportunity to teach, which will further equip their ministry skills. The study group model has distinct advantages.

Reflection Questions

Writing is one of the best ways to learn. In class, we take notes and write papers, and these methods are used to help us learn and retain the material. The same is true with the Word of God. Obviously, all the authors of Scripture were writers. This helped them better learn the Scriptures and also enabled them to more effectively teach it. As you reflect on God's Word, using the Bible Teacher's Guide, take time to write so you can similarly grow both in your learning and teaching.

1. How would you summarize the main points of the text/chapter? Write a brief summary.

2. What stood out to you most in the reading? Did any of the contents trigger any memories or experiences? If so, please share them.

3. What follow–up questions did you have about the reading? What parts did you not fully agree with?

4. What applications did you take from the reading, and how do you plan to implement them into your life?

5. Write several commitment statements: As a result of my time studying God's Word, I will . . .

6. What are some practical ways to pray as a result of studying the text? Spend some time ministering to the Lord through prayer.

Walking the Romans Road

How can a person be saved? From what is he saved? How can someone have eternal life? Scripture teaches that, after death, each person will spend eternity either in heaven or hell. How can a person go to heaven?

Paul said this to Timothy:

> You, however, must continue in the things you have learned and are confident about. You know who taught you and how from infancy you have known the holy writings, which are able to give you wisdom for salvation through faith in Christ Jesus.
> 2 Timothy 3:14-15

One of the reasons God gave us Scripture is to make us wise for salvation. This means that without it, nobody can know how to be saved.

Well then, how can a people be saved and what are they being saved from? A common method of sharing the good news of salvation is through the Romans Road. One of the great themes, not only of the Bible, but specifically of the book of Romans, is salvation. In Romans, the author, Paul, clearly details the steps we must take in order to be saved.

How can we be saved? What steps must we take?

Step One: We Must Accept that We Are Sinners

Romans 3:23 says, "For all have sinned and fall short of the glory of God." What does it mean to sin? The word sin means "to miss the mark." The mark we missed is reflecting God's image. When God created mankind in the Genesis narrative, he created man in the "image of God" (1:27). The "image of God" means many things, but most importantly it means we were made to be holy just as he is holy. Man was made moral. We were meant to reflect God's holiness in every way: the way we think, the way we talk, and the way we act. And any time we miss the mark in these areas, we commit sin.

Furthermore, we do not only sin when we commit a sinful act, such as lying, stealing, or cheating. We sin anytime we have a wrong heart motive. The greatest commandments in Scripture are to "Love the Lord your God with all your heart and to love your neighbor as yourself" (Matt 22:36-40, paraphrase). Whenever we don't love God supremely and love others as ourselves, we sin and fall short of the glory of God. For this reason, man is always in a state of sinning. Sadly, even if our actions are good, our heart is bad. I have never loved God with my whole heart, mind, and soul, and neither has anybody else. Therefore, we have all sinned and fall short of the glory of God (Rom 3:23). We have all missed the mark of God's holiness and we must accept this.

What's the next step?

Step Two: We Must Understand We Are Under the Judgment of God

Why are we under the judgment of God? It is because of our sins. Scripture teaches that God is not only a loving God, but he is also a just God. And his justice requires judgment for each of our sins. Romans 6:23 says, "For the payoff of sin is death."

A payoff or wage is something we earn. Every time we sin, we earn the wage of death. What is death? Death really means separation. In physical death, the body is separated from the spirit, but in spiritual death, man is separated from God. Man currently lives in a state of spiritual death (cf. Eph 2:1-3). We do not love God, obey him, or know him as we should. Therefore, man is in a state of death.

Moreover, on the day of our physical death, if we have not been saved, we will spend eternity separated from God in a very real hell. In hell, we will pay the wage for each of our sins. Therefore, in hell people will experience various degrees of punishment (cf. Lk 12:47-48). This places man in a very dangerous predicament—unholy and therefore under the judgment of God.

How should we respond to this? This leads us to our third step.

Step Three: We Must Recognize God Has Invited All to Accept His Free Gift of Salvation

Romans 6:23 does not stop at the wages of sin being death. It says, "For the payoff of sin is death, but the gift of God is eternal life in Christ Jesus our Lord." Because God loved everybody on the earth, he offered the free gift of eternal life, which anyone can receive through Jesus Christ.

Because it is a gift, it cannot be earned. We cannot work for it. Ephesians 2:8-9 says, "For by grace you are saved through faith, and this is not from yourselves, it is the gift of God; it is not from works, so that no one can boast."

Going to church, being baptized, giving to the poor, or doing any other righteous work does not save. Salvation is a gift that must be received from God. It is a gift that has been prepared by his effort alone.

How do we receive this free gift?

Step Four: We Must Believe Jesus Christ Died for Our Sins and Rose from the Dead

If we are going to receive this free gift, we must believe in God's Son, Jesus Christ. Because God loved us, cared for us, and didn't want us to be separated from him eternally, he sent his Son to die for our sins. Romans 5:8 says, "But God demonstrates his own love for us, in that while we were still sinners, Christ died for us." Similarly, John 3:16 says, "For this is the way God loved the world: He gave his one and only Son, so that everyone who believes in him will not perish but have eternal life." God so loved us that he gave his only Son for our sins.

Jesus Christ was a real, historical person who lived 2,000 years ago. He was born of a virgin. He lived a perfect life. He was put to death by the Romans and the Jews. And after he was buried, he rose again on the third day. In his death, he took our sins and God's wrath for those sins and gave us his perfect righteousness so we could be accepted by God. Second Corinthians 5:21 says, "God made the one who did not know sin to be sin for us, so that in him we would become the righteousness of God." God did all this so we could be saved from his wrath.

Christ's death satisfied the just anger of God over our sins. When God looked at Jesus on the cross, he saw us and our sins and therefore judged Jesus. And now, when God sees those of us who are saved, he sees his righteous Son and accepts us. In salvation, we have become the righteousness of God.

If we are going to be saved, if we are going to receive this free gift of salvation, we must believe in Christ's death, burial, and resurrection for our sins (cf. 1 Cor 15:3-5, Rom 10:9-10). Do you believe?

Step Five: We Must Confess Christ as Lord of Our Lives

Romans 10:9-10 says,

> Because if you confess with your mouth that Jesus is Lord and believe in your heart that God raised him from the dead, you will be saved. For with the heart one believes and thus has righteousness and with the mouth one confesses and thus has salvation.

Not only must we believe, but we must confess Christ as Lord of our lives. It is one thing to believe in Christ but another to follow Christ. Simple belief does not save. Christ must be our Lord. James said this: "...Even the demons believe that – and tremble with fear" (James 2:19), but the demons are not saved—Christ is not their Lord.

Another aspect of making Christ Lord is repentance. Repentance really means a change of mind that leads to a change of direction. Before we met Christ, we were living our own life and following our own sinful desires. But when we get saved, our mind and direction change. We start to follow Christ as Lord.

How do we make this commitment to the lordship of Christ so we can be saved? Paul said we must confess with our mouth "Jesus is Lord" as we believe in him. Romans 10:13 says, "For everyone who calls on the name of the Lord will be saved."

If you admit that you are a sinner and understand you are under God's wrath because of it; if you believe Jesus Christ is the Son of God, that he died on the cross for your sins, and rose from the dead for your salvation; if you are ready to turn from your sin and cling to Christ as Lord, you can be saved.

If this is your heart, then you can pray this prayer and commit to following Christ as your Lord.

> Dear heavenly Father, I confess I am a sinner and have fallen short of your glory, what you made me for. I believe

Jesus Christ died on the cross to pay the penalty for my sins and rose from the dead so I can have eternal life. I am turning away from my sin and accepting you as my Lord and Savior. Come into my life and change me. Thank you for your gift of salvation.

Scripture teaches that if you truly accept Christ as your Lord, then you are a new creation. Second Corinthians 5:17 says, "So then, if anyone is in Christ, he is a new creation; what is old has passed away – look, what is new has come!" God has forgiven your sins (1 John 1:9), he has given you his Holy Spirit (Rom 8:15), and he is going to disciple you and make you into the image of his Son (cf. Rom 8:29). He will never leave you nor forsake you (Heb 13:5), and he will complete the work he has begun in your life (Phil 1:6). In heaven, angels and saints are rejoicing because of your commitment to Christ (Lk 15:7).

Praise God for his great salvation! May God keep you in his hand, empower you through the Holy Spirit, train you through mature believers, and use you to build his kingdom! "He who calls you is trustworthy, and he will in fact do this" (1 Thess 5:24). God bless you!

Coming Soon

Praise the Lord for your interest in studying and teaching God's Word. If God has blessed you through the BTG series, please partner with us in petitioning God to greatly use this series to encourage and build his Church. Also, please consider leaving an Amazon review and signing up for free book promotions. By doing this, you help spread the "Word." Thanks for your partnership in the gospel from the first day until now (Phil 1:4-5).

<u>Available:</u>
First Peter
Theology Proper
Building Foundations for a Godly Marriage
Colossians
God's Battle Plan for Purity
Nehemiah
Philippians
The Perfections of God
The Armor of God
Ephesians
Abraham
Finding a Godly Mate
1 Timothy
The Beatitudes
Equipping Small Group Leaders
2 Timothy
Jacob

About the Author

Greg Brown earned his MA in religion and MA in teaching from Trinity International University, a MRE from Liberty University, and a PhD in theology from Louisiana Baptist University. He has served over sixteen years in pastoral ministry and currently serves as a chaplain and professor at Handong Global University, teaching pastor at Handong International Congregation, and as a Navy Reserve chaplain.

Greg married his lovely wife, Tara Jayne, in 2006, and they have one daughter, Saiyah Grace. He enjoys going on dates with his wife, playing with his daughter, reading, writing, studying in coffee shops, working out, and following the NBA and UFC. His pursuit in life, simply stated, is "to know God and to be found faithful by Him."

To connect with Greg, please follow at http://www.pgregbrown.com.

Notes

1 Grudem, Wayne A. Bible Doctrine: Essential Teachings of the Christian Faith (p. 364). Zondervan. Kindle Edition.

2 Barclay, W. (2002). The Letter to the Romans (3rd ed. fully rev. & updated, p. 55). Louisville, KY; London: Westminster John Knox Press.

3 MacArthur, J., & Mayhue, R. (Eds.). (2017). Biblical Doctrine: A Systematic Summary of Bible Truth (p. 748). Wheaton, IL: Crossway.

4 Grudem, Wayne A. Bible Doctrine: Essential Teachings of the Christian Faith (p. 368). Zondervan. Kindle Edition.

5 Accessed 9/1/20 from https://www.gotquestions.org/covenant-theology.html

6 Ryrie, C. C. (1999). Basic Theology: A Popular Systematic Guide to Understanding Biblical Truth (p. 464). Chicago, IL: Moody Press.

7 MacArthur, J., & Mayhue, R. (Eds.). (2017). Biblical Doctrine: A Systematic Summary of Bible Truth (p. 748). Wheaton, IL: Crossway.

8 Grudem, Wayne A. Bible Doctrine: Essential Teachings of the Christian Faith (p. 367). Zondervan. Kindle Edition.

9 Grudem, W. A. (2004). Systematic theology: an introduction to biblical doctrine (p. 922). Leicester, England; Grand Rapids, MI: Inter-Varsity Press; Zondervan Pub. House.

10 MacArthur, J. F., Jr. (1995). 1 Timothy (p. 111). Chicago: Moody Press.

11 MacArthur, J. F., Jr. (1995). 1 Timothy (p. 107). Chicago: Moody Press.

12 Hughes, R. K., & Chapell, B. (2000). 1 & 2 Timothy and Titus: to guard the deposit (p. 83). Wheaton, IL: Crossway Books.

13 MacArthur, J. F., Jr. (1995). 1 Timothy (p. 130). Chicago: Moody Press.

14 MacArthur, J. F., Jr. (1995). 1 Timothy (p. 130). Chicago: Moody Press.

15 Aaron, Daryl. Understanding Theology in 15 Minutes a Day: Baker Publishing Group. Kindle Edition.

16 Aaron, Daryl. Understanding Theology in 15 Minutes a Day: Baker Publishing Group. Kindle Edition.

17 Ryrie, C. C. (1999). Basic Theology: A Popular Systematic Guide to Understanding Biblical Truth (pp. 488–489). Chicago, IL: Moody Press.
18 Ryrie, C. C. (1999). Basic Theology: A Popular Systematic Guide to Understanding Biblical Truth (p. 489). Chicago, IL: Moody Press.
19 Ryrie, C. C. (1999). Basic Theology: A Popular Systematic Guide to Understanding Biblical Truth (p. 490). Chicago, IL: Moody Press.
20 Grudem, W. A. (2004). Systematic theology: an introduction to biblical doctrine (p. 967). Leicester, England; Grand Rapids, MI: Inter-Varsity Press; Zondervan Pub. House.
21 Ryrie, C. C. (1999). Basic Theology: A Popular Systematic Guide to Understanding Biblical Truth (p. 491). Chicago, IL: Moody Press.
22 Ryrie, C. C. (1999). Basic Theology: A Popular Systematic Guide to Understanding Biblical Truth (p. 491). Chicago, IL: Moody Press.
23 MacArthur, J., & Mayhue, R. (Eds.). (2017). Biblical Doctrine: A Systematic Summary of Bible Truth (p. 786). Wheaton, IL: Crossway.
24 MacArthur, J., & Mayhue, R. (Eds.). (2017). Biblical Doctrine: A Systematic Summary of Bible Truth (p. 788). Wheaton, IL: Crossway.
25 Grudem, W. A. (2004). Systematic theology: an introduction to biblical doctrine (p. 989). Leicester, England; Grand Rapids, MI: Inter-Varsity Press; Zondervan Pub. House.
26 Aaron, Daryl. Understanding Theology in 15 Minutes a Day: How can I know God? Baker Publishing Group. Kindle Edition.
27 Grudem, W. A. (2004). Systematic theology: an introduction to biblical doctrine (p. 991). Leicester, England; Grand Rapids, MI: Inter-Varsity Press; Zondervan Pub. House.
28 Aaron, Daryl. Understanding Theology in 15 Minutes a Day: How can I know God? Baker Publishing Group. Kindle Edition.
29 https://www.christiancourier.com/articles/477-what-are-transubstantiation-and-consubstantiation
30 Aaron, Daryl. Understanding Theology in 15 Minutes a Day: How can I know God? Baker Publishing Group. Kindle Edition.
31 Accessed 6/6/2020 from https://simplyputpodcast.com/four-views-of-the-lords-supper/
32 Hughes, R. K. (1999). John: that you may believe (p. 117). Wheaton, IL: Crossway Books.
33 Grudem, W. A. (2004). Systematic theology: an introduction to biblical doctrine (pp. 896–897). Leicester, England; Grand Rapids, MI: Inter-Varsity Press; Zondervan Pub. House.
34 MacArthur, J., & Mayhue, R. (Eds.). (2017). Biblical Doctrine: A Systematic Summary of Bible Truth (p. 795). Wheaton, IL: Crossway.

[35] Grudem, W. A. (2004). _Systematic theology: an introduction to biblical doctrine_ (p. 868). Leicester, England; Grand Rapids, MI: Inter-Varsity Press; Zondervan Pub. House.

[36] Grudem, W. A. (2004). Systematic theology: an introduction to biblical doctrine (p. 868). Leicester, England; Grand Rapids, MI: Inter-Varsity Press; Zondervan Pub. House.